This edition published in 2002 by

TODTRI BOOK PUBLISHERS
254 West 31st Street
New York, NY 10001-2813
Fax: (212) 695-6984
E-mail: info@todtri.com

Visit us on the web!
www.todtri.com <http://www.todtri.com>

Printed and bound in Italy

ISBN 1-57717-303-1

Front cover:
**Bonaparte on the bridge of Arcola,
on November 17, 1796**
Antoine-Jean Gros (1771-1835), details.
Musée du château de Versailles
Pages 6/7:
**The Czar Alexander I introduces the Kalmuks,
the Cossacks and the Baskirs of the russian army
to Napoleon, on July 9, 1807**
Pierre Nolasque Bergeret (1782-1863)
Musée du château de Versailles
Back cover :
**The Coronation of Emperor Napoleon,
on December 2, 1804**
Louis David (1748-1825), details.
Musée du Louvre
Inside front and back pages:
**The award of the first "Legion of Honour"
crosses inside the Invalides Church,
on July 15, 1804**
Jean-Baptiste Debret (1768-1848)
Page 11:
The imperial coat of arms

Photographic credits:

R.M.N.: 1, 2/3, 6/7, 14/15, 17, 29, 41, 42/43, 45, 46/47, 48/49, 60/61, 62/63, 67, 69, 70/71, 74/75, 78/79, 81, 82/83, 86/87, 95, 98/99, 104/105, 106/107, 134/135, 136;
Tallandier: 11, 19, 21, 33, 39, 85, 89;
Musée de la Monnaie: 55, 56, 57;
Bulloz: 23.

Documents:

Clavreuil: 120-128;
Martinez: 13, 36/37, 72/73, 76/77, 90, 91, 100/101, 102/103, 108/109, 111, 112, 129;
Michèle Polak: 50/51;
Bernard Quintin: 116/117;
Author's Collection: 52/53, 65, 93, 131;
Molière Archives: 27, 31, 34.

Text: Eric Ledru
Contribution: F. B.

NAPOLEON
THE VISIONARY CONQUEROR

Eric Ledru

Foreword
Jean Tulard

TODTRI

NAPOLEON

FOREWORD

Another book about Napoleon, you would say. But a book you will love to read and read again, to open at random to skim through a chapter or to study a picture. It is a book which will make you dream, but also one you will use as a reference for names and dates.

Eric Ledru has given his work an original subtitle: "The visionary conqueror." Napoleon was indeed one of the greatest conquerors in history, in the tradition of Alexander the Great and Gengis Khan.

Empires, like civilizations, are mortal and the "Grand Empire" which had encompassed a part of western Europe came to know the fate of its predecessors.

But Eric Ledru is right to speak of a "visionary" conqueror. Altough the domination of Europe by Napoleon was short-lived, it left a lasting mark. The Emperor enjoyed reminding Las Cases of it in St Helena.

He dismantled the feudal world symbolized by the Holy Roman Empire in Germany. In Italy (especially in the north), on German soil (with the model-kingdom of Westphalia), in Poland, in Spain (where Napoleon abolished the Inquisition), without forgetting the annexed countries, everywhere the vestiges of what would be called from then on the Ancien Régime disappeared. The old aristocracy lost ground to the bourgeoisie, capitalism arose after the disappearance of the guilds, civil law was reformed by the Napoleonic Code and the peasants were set free.

The idea of Europe too came to life. The map of the Old Continent was simplified: fewer states in Germany after the declaration of 1803, the beginnings of unification in Italy, and the birth of national aspirations in Spain. Napoleon cleverly knew how to take credit for it in the Mémorial de Sainte-Hélène.

Never have subsequent events so convincingly proven the vanquished to be right. The entire nineteenth century and much of our twentieth are contained in that napoleonic epic tale which Eric Ledru narrates with talent and thoughtfulness.

Jean TULARD

CONTENTS

FOREWORD: JEAN TULARD — 9

INTRODUCTION — 12

NAPOLEON BUONAPARTE: 1769-1789 — 18-25

A corsican childhood: 1769-1778 — 18
The rebellious island — 18
The Buonapartes — 18
The first years — 20

A French youth: 1778-1789 — 22
At Brienne — 22
In Paris — 23
Garrison life — 24

THE SOLDIER OF FORTUNE: 1789-1804 — 26-67

An Adventurer in the Revolution:1789-1796 — 26
The corsican Patriot: 1789-1791 — 26
The Great Hope: 1789-1791 — 26
The end of a dream: 1791-1793 — 30
The young general: 1793-1796 — 32
In the service of Robespierre: 1793-1794 — 32
In the service of Barras: 1794-1796 — 35

The apprenticeship of Power: 1796-1804 — 40
The beginnings of an epic: 1796-1799 — 40
The Campaign of Italy: 1796-1797 — 40
The mirages of Egypt: 1798-1799 — 44

Towards the Coronation: 1799-1804 — 52
Brumaire Year VIII (November 9 and 10, 1799) — 52
The reorganization of the country: 1800-1802 — 55
Consul for life: 1802-1804 — 64

THE EMPEROR: 1804-1815 — 68-111

The visionary conqueror: 1804-1812 — 68
The pinnacle of power: 1804-1807 — 68
The period of conquests — 68
The Empire in 1807 — 78
After Tilsit: 1808-1812 — 80
The Logic of expansion — 80
The weaknesses of the napoleonic "system" — 94

The end of the Epic times: 1812-1815 — 96
The initial setbacks: 1812-1813 — 96
The Campaign of Russia: 1812 — 96
The Campaign of Germany: 1813 — 100
The Long Agony: 1814-1815 — 104
The Campaign of France: 1814 — 104
The island of Elba and the Hundred Days: 1841-1815 — 108

ANNEXES — 113-128

EPILOGUE: 1815-1821 — 130-131
St Helena and the Legend — 130

INTRODUCTION

St Helena is a gloomy and wind-battered volcanic crag, lost in the Atlantic Ocean, its landscape desolate and barren of vegetation. Jamestown, the capital of the island, is also its only city. This bleak rock would never have risen to fame, had Napoleon, a man whose destiny would mark forever Europe and the world, not died there on May 5, 1821.

His death was without grandeur after a life devoted to the pursuit of glory. Count de Las Cases bears witness to that in his diary, which would become the *Mémorial de Sainte-Hélène*.

Let him tell it in his own words:

"Saturday October 26, 1816.

They said the Emperor was in great pain. He had me brought to his room. I found him there, his head wrapped in a handkerchief, in his armchair pulled close to the large fire that he had ordered lit. 'Which ill is the most vivid, which pain the sharpest?' *he asked. I answered that it was the one at the moment.* 'Well then, it is a toothache!' *he told me. He had a terrible inflammation indeed; his right cheek was very swollen and very red. I was then alone with him. I started to heat up a piece of flannel and a towel which he alternately applied to the afflicted area, and he said it made him feel much better. Added to all that were an irritated cough and the yawning and shivering that precede a fever [...].*

The doctor came in and found he had got the first signs of a fever. The Emperor spent the rest of the day in this way, suffering at times from a very intense pain, going back and forth between his chair and his couch, and filling the periods of suffering with conversation on different subjects [...].

In the evening the pain had subsided, and the Emperor was able to fall asleep; he must have been suffering a great deal, his whole appearance had changed.

Sunday 27.

The Emperor spent the whole day on the couch or in his chair next to the fire. He had got little sleep, was in great pain as yesterday and had not eaten. His headache and toothache were particularly sharp, and the swelling had not gone down. He used again the flannel and the hot towels, as he had the day before, which, he told me when I came in, had done him so much good yesterday. I began heating them up and applying them again; he seemed moved by this, sometimes resting his arm on my shoulders, repeating often to me: 'Dear friend, you are doing me so much good!' *With the pain calmed down, he dozed off a few moments; then, reopening his eyes:* 'Did I sleep long, *he said to me,* did you get bored to death?' *and he called me then his Friar Hospitaler, the Maltese Knight of St Helena. As he was in pain again, more intensely than ever, he called for the doctor who found him feverish; the chills from the day before had come back and he had to draw closer to the fire.*

Monday 28.

Water in general is rather scarce in Longwood; but recently this scarcity has markedly increased, and it is quite a task today to provide the Emperor with a bath. We are not any better in other areas of medical assistance: yesterday the doctor spoke to the Emperor of drugs, instruments, necessary treatments; but to each one of them, he was adding:

'- Unfortunately, there are none on the island.

- But, *the Emperor said to him,* in sending us here, did not they commit themselves to keep us always in good health?'

In fact the smallest and the most necessary things were lacking. To have his bed warmed, the Emperor could find no other way than to have holes

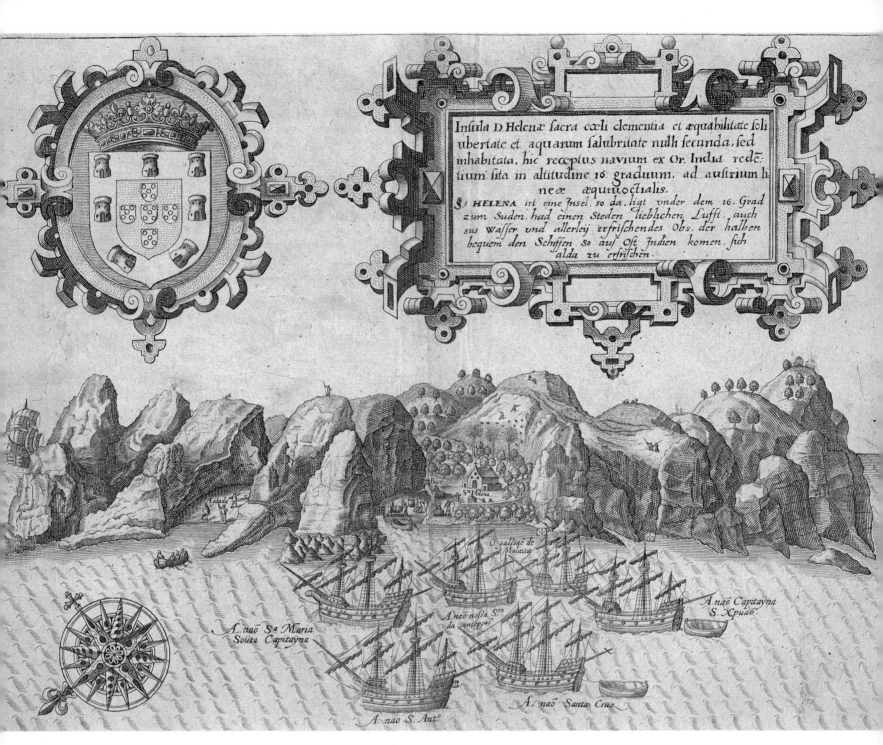

Insula D. Helenæ sacra cœli clementia et æquabilitate soli ubertate et aquarum salubritate nulli secunda, sed inhabitata, hic receptus navium ex Or. India redetium sita in altitudine 16. graduum. ad austrium hnex æquinoctialis.

S. HELENA ist eine Insel, so da ligt under dem 16. Grad zum Suden, had einen Steden lieblichen Lufft, auch sus Waffer und allerley erfrischendes Obs, der halben bequem den Schiffen so auß Oft Indien komen, sich alda zu erfrischen.

punched in one of the large silver globes used to keep plates warm on the dining table, and to fill it with hot coals. For the past two nights he had been unnecessarily craving for some spirits which could warm up a few comforting drinks.

The Emperor continued to suffer the whole day; his cheek remained swollen but less painful... Like yesterday, he found himself forced to retire early. He must have had a fever because he was chilled to the bone. He had only eaten a soup since the day before and felt dizzy spells. He considered his bed to be poorly made, with the blankets in disorder; everything was going wrong, he said, and he tried to make sense of the whole situation as much as he could by remarking that everything around him was geared to him being in good health, and that everyone would prove inexperienced and no doubt unprepared, should he ever fall seriously ill.

Thursday 31.

The weather had turned beautiful; today the temperature was delightful. The Emperor had been confined to his room for the past six days; weary of the monotony of his pains, he decided, as he said, to break the doctor's rules. He went out, but he felt weak and could hardly walk. He called for his carriage and went for a short ride. He was silent and sad. He was suffering a great deal, particularly from the sores covering his lips.

Summary of July, August, September, October.

From now on the usual report would not be long; three sentences could possibly sum it up:

Utter torment.

Absolute isolation.

Certain destruction.

The rest of Napoleon's life will only be a long and cruel agony.

St Helena

Although this island was very early a convenient port of call for the transoceanic voyages made by the great maritime powers, it had not the appeal of a new Cythera: this 17th century engraving perfectly illustrates the dismal character of the place. Historical documents note that there were fresh air and abundant water: Napoleon would not have shared that view.

Portuguese engraving of 1615.

We saw that the arrival of the new governor had been for us an ominous sign for the future. It took him only a few days to set up his sinister program. Soon the torments, the insults which he passed along or inflicted himself, were at their peak. He set the inhabitants against us; he heaped the most ridiculous abuse on us... The attacks on Napoleon were incessant, torments constant. A day did not go by without a new affront.

During that period the Emperor's health had constantly and seriously declined; thought so robust, his body, which had endured so many trials, which has been spared by so many hardships, so much fatigue, which had been supported by victories and glory, was now bent under infirmities that left him vulnerable to the cruelty of others. Each day revealed some new discomfort, signs of fever, serious swellings, symptoms of scurvy, constant colds; the lines of his face deteriorated, his walk became burdened, his legs swelled, etc. It broke our hearts to see him nearing his inevitable demise; all our care could do nothing for him.

He had given up riding a horse for a long time now, and almost gave up riding in his carriage as well; he even seldom ventured out, and found himself almost completely restricted to his apartments. From then on, he no longer continued with sustained or regular work, he only dictated to us between long intervals and on spur-of-the-moment subjects. He was spending the better part of the day alone in his room, leafing through a few books, or rather doing nothing. Those who had gauged his formidable faculties could appreciate the strength of character he needed to quietly endure the overwhelming weight of such boredom, of such an unbearable life. As far as we were concerned, there was always the same serene countenance, the same steady character, the same bite, the same freedom of spirit, sometimes even the same cheerfulness and jesting; but upon having a closer look at his private life, it was easy to notice that he was no longer concerned with the future, neither meditating over the past nor worried about the present. He now passively obeyed the physical laws of nature in a complete distaste for life, its end perhaps his secret desire..."

Was this the man of the campaigns of Italy, Marengo and Austerlitz? The one who had conquered or subjugated Europe, and whose momentum fizzled out in

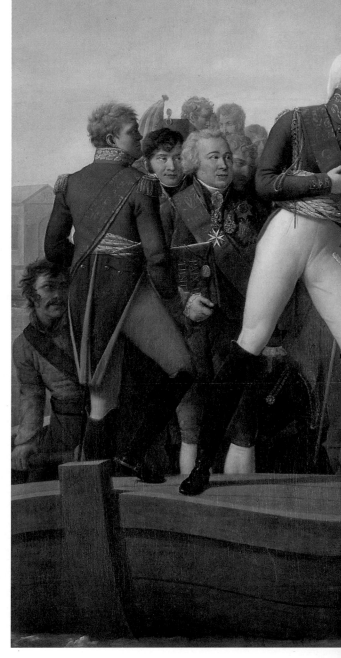

the Russian steppes? Was it the same one who, only nine years ago, had met Czar Alexander I on a raft at Tilsit?

It was June 25, 1807. A few days earlier, the Grand Army had shattered the Russian forces of Bennigsen, forcing him to ask for an armistice. Frederick William III of Prussia had taken refuge in Russia, begging the Czar to welcome him. France was seizing all the states to the west of the Elbe river. The Prussia of Frederick the Great did not exist anymore.

The day following the battle, Napoleon had addressed his victorious soldiers:

"Soldiers,

On June 5, the Russian army attacked our camp. The enemy misinterpreted our passiveness then, and realized too late that our rest was the lion's repose, which they now regret to have disturbed.

In the days at Guttstadt, at Heilsberg and at the one forever memorable of Friedland, in ten days of campaign, we took 120 cannons, 7 flags, killed,

wounded or took prisoner 60,0000 Russians, seized the enemy's army storage depots, hospitals, ambulances, Koenigsberg Place, the 300 hundred buildings that were in that port, filled with all kinds of munitions, and 160,000 rifles which England had sent to arm our enemies.

From the banks of the Vistula to the Niemen's ones, we went with the swiftness of the eagle. At Austerlitz you celebrated the anniversary of the coronation, this year you have fittingly celebrated the anniversary of the battle of Marengo which ended the war of the Second Coalition.

Frenchmen! You have showed your true worth, and I am proud of you. You will return to France wearing laurels after having obtained a glorious peace which is guaranteed to last. It is time for our country to live in peace, sheltered from England's evil influence. I shall reward you to show my gratitude and the extent of the love I feel for you.

The imperial camp at Tilsit on June 22, 1807."

An eye-witness, the Imperial Guard Coignet, has left us this striking description:

"Our officers informed us that a raft was being prepared in the middle of the river for Alexander's reception, and that the two sovereigns would have a private discussion to conclude a peace agreement. Our hearts filled with joy, at last it was over!

Our leaders came among us to make sure that nothing in our appearance was amiss, that our ranks were well-formed and our leather gear well polished. When everything was ready, around eleven o'clock in the morning, we went down to the river. There, waiting for us, was the most beautiful sight any man would ever see. In the middle of the Niemen river was a large raft, festooned with broad and magnificent tapestries, and with a pavilion on its left-hand side. A richly decorated boat was moored on each bank of the river. Napoleon arrived around one in the afternoon and boarded with his staff one of these two boats, manned by sailors of the guard. Alexander took the other one on the opposite shore.

The farewell of Napoleon and Alexander I at Tilsit, on July 9, 1807

When he met Czar Alexander on the raft anchored in the middle of the Niemen river, Napoleon could claim to have subdued Europe. Only Britain remained undefeated. At 38 years of age, he was at the height of his glory. His relationship with the Czar, then 30, was at once excellent. "He pleased me and I liked him for it…" he would confide. The separation was painful. However, an increasing rift grew between them that would last until their final conflict.
Giocachino Giuseppe Serangelli (1768-1856), Salon of 1810
Musée du château de Versailles.

At a given signal, the two emperors set out. They each had the same distance to travel and the same number of stairs to climb to reach the platform on the raft. But our Napoleon was the first to arrive. Once the two sovereigns had reached the meeting place, we saw them embrace as if they were two brothers. The troops, gathered on both shores, shouted out frenzied cheers. The whole valley resounded with them.

After the meeting, which was very long, each emperor withdrew to his own side... The next day the guard set up ranks three deep on either side of the main street in Tilsit, and Napoleon went out to meet Alexander up to the banks of the river. The King of Prussia was nowhere to be found. What a beautiful sight! These two emperors, these princes, these marshals, all clothed in their richest attire. The Emperor of Russia, passing in front of us said to our Colonel Frédéric, from the first regiment:

'- You have some smart looking troops there, Colonel!

- And good soldiers too, Sire, Frédéric added.

- I know, Alexander responded.'

The king of Prussia came a little later to join the two emperors and Napoleon treated his two hosts to an impressive revue of his Guards as well as of the third army corps under the command of Marshal Davout. We were in full parade dress, as brilliant as if in Paris. The marshal's troops were no less splendid. Napoleon could rightly be proud."

Napoleon was the real hero of these days at Tilsit. His flags were flying from the Atlantic to the Niemen and he was in a position to have his way with his two defeated adversaries. He was above all able to convince the Czar to join forces with him against England. Alexander, young, sentimental, mystic and mercurial, distressed by the defeat, was seduced by the conqueror who forgave him everything and offered him an alliance as well as his friendship. Out of self-interest, but also because he felt attracted by the genius of a man who had thrown Europe into confusion, the Czar gave in to the persuasive arguments of his former enemy. Moreover, he vowed so deep a friendship to him that it would turn into an undying hatred the very day it was betrayed.

In 1807 Alexander was 30 years old and Napoleon 38. Meeting each night in private, they were remapping the world. What were the contents of these confidential "chats" between the two masters of Europe? A letter from Napoleon to Alexander dated February 2, 1808, helps give us an idea:

"Your majesty must already have seen the latest discussions in the English Parliament and the decision there to press for an all-out war. It is now therefore only through bold and wide-ranging decisions that we can reach peace and consolidate our system. Let your Majesty increase and strengthen his army. I shall wholeheartedly give your Majesty all the help and assistance I can possibly give. I hold no feelings of jealousy towards Russia, I only wish its glory, prosperity and expansion.

An army of 50,000 men, Russian, French, with perhaps a few Austrians, which would head for Asia via Constantinople, would not have reached yet the banks of the Euphrates river that England would tremble with fear and be at the mercy of the Continent. I am well positioned in Dalmatia, and so is your Majesty on the Danube. A month after we have agreed about it, we could be on the Bosphorus banks. The blow would be felt in India, and England would surrender.

Everything can be decided and signed before March 15. By the first of May, our troops could be in Asia. Then the English, threatened in India, chased out of the Levant, will be crushed under the weight of these important events. Your majesty and I would have preferred the sweetness of peace and to spend our lives in our vast empires, striving to make our people happy thanks to the benefits of a long-lasting peace and of a good administration; but the enemies of mankind do not want that. We must surpass ourselves, in spite of ourselves. Wisdom and politics dictate to do what destiny commands and to go where the irresistible course of events leads us. This host of pygmies, who do not want to see that current events are such that comparisons must be sought in history and not in the popular press of the last century, will then yield and follow the direction Your Majesty and I will have decided; the Russian people will rejoice with the glory, riches and good fortune which will result from these great events.

In these few lines, your Majesty, I express all of my feelings. The work done at Tilsit will determine the fate of the world. Perhaps, both your Majesty and I,

being a little fainthearted, would tend to prefer the current peaceful situation to something even better and more perfect. But since England does not want it that way, we must acknowledge that the era of great changes and great events has come."

The man who wrote these lines was at the height of his power. Italy and Germany had already submitted to him, Austria did not dare rebel, and he was preparing to invade Spain. Russia was his ally and the Czar claimed to be his friend. Great Britain alone still dared to resist him with the strength born of despair. Everything was going his way. Yet, nine years later, there he was, wandering on the rock of St Helena, driven to despair, worn down by the sustained exercise of power, expecting nothing more from life, relinquishing himself to the sickness that was slowly

sapping him and contemplating the highlights of his extraordinary destiny. Young officer on the eve of the Revolution, adventurer in Corsica, conqueror of Italy, master of Egypt, First Consul, Emperor…

His entire epic story lasted less than twenty years. He confided to Las Cases, referring to a man who had reached thirty:

"At that age, […] I had made all my conquests, I was ruling the world, I had calmed the storm, unified opposing sides, rallied a nation, created a government, an empire; I was just lacking the title of emperor… I was spoiled, I have to admit, I always commanded. As soon as I made my debut, I found myself rich with power, and circumstances and my strengths were such that, as soon as I was given command, I no longer knew either masters or laws…"

The life of Napoleon in eight hats

This kind of charade allowed the artist to recount the glorious and tragic times of the empire without representing the Emperor himself, at a time when the restored monarchy worried about the place the "Little Corporal" was taking in the people's hearts.
Baron Charles de Steuben (1788-1856)
Musée de la Malmaison.

NAPOLEON BUONAPARTE

1769-1789

A corsican childhood: 1769-1778

The rebellious island

When Napoleon was born on August 15, 1769, Corsica had been French for only one year and a few months. Louis XV had officially bought it from Genoa in May 1768, pleased to gain possession of an island with great strategic value in that region of the Mediterranean. In all his grand political calculations, the king of France had however neglected an important detail: the Corsicans had absolutely no desire to become French, as their long held aspiration was to become independent.

Their political, military and spiritual leader was Pascal Paoli, affectionately nicknamed "Babbo." Born in 1725, he had to follow in 1739 his father, a die-hard patriot, into exile to Naples, where he studied. In 1755 he returned to Corsica where he was proclaimed general of the nation. He had thus been playing an eminent part in his homeland since the middle of the 18th century, and could rightly claim to be the soul of the corsican resistance. Paoli had long struggled against the Genoese domination and managed to "liberate" the interior of the island by pushing their garrisons to the coastal towns.

Arguing that Corsicans were not consulted about ceding their country to France, Paoli rallied his partisans and declared war on Louis XV. The few French troops which landed on the island were driven to the sea, and it took nearly a year of fighting before Paoli was defeated at Ponto Nuovo on May 8, 1769. He managed to escape, and exiled himself to England where he would wait for an opportunity to reappear on the front stage.

The Buonapartes

Corsican patriots were in total disarray: what could they do against the tremendous power of their invading neighbour? Retreat to the mountains? Take to the bush hoping for better days? Some did so. Charles Buonaparte, a former lieutenant of Paoli, chose to collaborate, and in doing so decided the destiny of his son and of millions of men.

The need to feed his family as well as his scheming personality helped him make the choice that he would not come to regret. France pardoned all of the rebels and the Buonapartes —Charles and his wife Laetitia— were able to return to Ajaccio for the birth of their second son, named Napoleon in honor of an uncle who had died two years before. The eldest son, Joseph, was born in 1768. Other children would follow over the years: Lucien (1775), Elisa (1777), Louis (1778), Pauline (1780), Caroline (1782) and Jérôme (1783).

They lived in Malerba Street ("Weed Street") in a house shared with a few cousins, including the Pozzo di Borgo family. A serious feud divided the members of the two clans who often fought, at least verbally, over the most trifling matters.

The Buonaparte family, even if it were of relatively modest means (although it owned three houses, vineyards and a mill) could nevertheless behave very arrogantly. Originally from Tuscany, but settled in Ajaccio for several centuries, it could lay claim to a certain nobility. "Madame Laetitia," as she would be called later, was the guiding spirit of the family: it was

Maria Laetitia Ramolino, Madame Charles Buonaparte

Charles, the father, played a modest role in the Buonaparte family. The moving spirit was Laetitia, the mother of the future emperor. It was under her implacable authority that the apprentice dictator would spend his childhood.
Miniature on ivory.

19

under her firm and implacable authority that the future Emperor would live his first years. The father, however, held a less important place in the life of the family: a lawyer at the tribunal of Ajaccio, a connoisseur of pretty women and an inveterate gambler, he was scheming brilliantly for his own success and his family's one, borrowing money to keep up his status and feed his family. The French, once his sworn enemies, had soon become his best friends. The governor of Corsica, the Marquis de Marbeuf, was naturally admitted into the intimacy of the Buonaparte family, and if we are to believe certain malicious rumors, into Madame Laetitia's one as well.

Laetitia had indeed a lot to do to raise her brood. Charles' income being meager despite his distinguished status (he had been appointed assessor for the royal judicial region of Ajaccio), she had to watch her budget and avoid any waste.

"You will be poor, but it is better to have a beautiful drawing room, rich clothes, a fine horse and to keep up appearances —and then after to eat bread at home..." she would teach her eight children.

She never parted with her frugal habits which will be profusely derided later on.

"I have seven or eight sovereigns who may come back home one day" she explained to her friends during the Empire, to justify the savings made on her million pounds of revenue. They must have viewed her with a mixture of sympathy and jealousy: the Emperor's mother and her petty economies! This mania puzzled the aristocracy of the old European courts whose expensive life style was second nature. But Madame Laetitia knew the shifting sands of destiny, and what followed was to prove her right.

The first years

A puny child by nature and throughout his adolescence, Napoleon would however soon gain enough strength to be able, helped by his quarrelsome nature, to give a thrashing to his older brother and his playmates on a regular basis. His first education was not too much neglected: after attending classes with the Beguine nuns in Ajaccio, he was sent to Father Recco who taught him the rudiments of calculus —for which he had a natural aptitude— of reading and writing (in Corsican dialect), for which he was less gifted. When remembering this difficult period much later, Madame Laetitia would confide:

"At the beginning of his studies, Napoleon was the child of mine who gave me the least hope; it would take him a long time before having any success. When he finally received a good assessment from his teachers, he eagerly brought it home to me; after having shown me the report, he placed it on a chair and triumphantly sat down on it."

Anecdotes are plentiful, and more or less true, about the first signs of his domineering character: but it is undeniable that very character soon made him destined for a military career, while his brother Joseph would be off to the seminary.

Anxious to make best use of his French connections as well as to spare the family fortune the cost of educating his sons, Charles Buonaparte thought of sending them to study in France, where they would be taken on by the royal administration as humble scholarship students.

These projects were encouraged by the accommodating Monsieur de Marbeuf who was not satisfied enough with looking after Charles' interests, but wanted to take care of his children's future as well. The father of Napoleon, with the help of his protector, had got himself elected as a noble delegate from the States of Corsica to Versailles. He took advantage of the trip to bring his sons with him, leaving them on the way with the bishop of Autun, Monseigneur de Marbeuf, the governor's brother. Napoleon would wait there to be sent to a military academy which would accept him, while his father would work the ministerial back rooms to find him a place.

Thus, at the end of December 1778, the future Emperor left his native island in the company of his father and brother Joseph. At the mere age of nine, he left Corsica he loved so much, his mother and his childhood, everything that had counted for him until then. A foreign country was waiting for him, the language of which he did not speak, a country which had been for a long time, in his child's mind brought up on his mother's stories, the hated oppressor of his corsican homeland.

The first known portrait of Napoleon Buonaparte

This profile, probably close to the model, was painted from life by one of his classmates at Brienne, in 1783. Napoleon will relate how shocked her mother was when she saw him again during a visit to the military academy.

Mio Caro Amico
Buonaparte
Pontornino d. 1785
Tommom

21

A French youth: 1778-1789

It is nevertheless a French education that Napoleon Buonaparte will receive, first in secondary school in Autun, then at the military academy in Brienne, and finally in Paris.

The future Emperor's stay in Autun lasted only a few months (January to May 1779). His father had gone on to Paris, where he laid siege to the various administrative departments, to secure a place for his son. Napoleon himself was more than eager to leave the school in Autun where he was the target of constant mockery by his classmates who, on the other hand, had well received his brother Joseph. The administrative intrigues of Charles finally bore fruit: in the spring of 1779, the war ministry informed him that his son had been given a place in Brienne: Napoleon went there in May of that same year, while Joseph stayed in Autun to follow his seminary studies.

At Brienne

The little Corsican did not know how to win the heart of his French schoolmates; besides, he made no effort to that extent, suffering from his exile and taking refuge in an irritable timidity. He barely spoke the language of his classmates, and his physical appearance, along with his quick-tempered nature, made him the target of their mockery. His first name especially, pronounced in Corsican, inspired their jokes:

"Napolione! Na-paille-au-nez!" (straw in the nose).

Wrapped in his pride and hiding as best as he could his wounded self-esteem, Napoleon felt all the more hostile to France than he found French people most unpleasant. The legend of old Paoli was taking on an almost mystical dimension in his eyes; the memory of the great corsican leader was seldom leaving him. He was idolizing him so much that one day, to one of his professors who had foolishly asked him:

"How did it happen that you were defeated? You had Paoli, who was supposed to be such a good general!"

He responded sharply: "Yes sir, he was, and I would like to be like him!"

He had few friends. Bourrienne was his closest confidant and he was promising him, during his bouts of despair:

"I shall do as much harm as I can to your French people!"

It was during these years that he truly forged his character, which went from imperious to domineering. His role model was Paoli, and he dreamed of fighting by his side—as his father had done in the past before betraying the Cause—and, perhaps, of succeeding him one day. At the age of ten, Napoleon Buonaparte was imagining no other future than that of the liberator of a Corsica oppressed by those who were oppressing him. His own misery was merging with the one of his homeland, uniting them with a bond that was growing stronger every day. These dreams of an unhappy child, far from his own family, made him a rebellious, aggressive, and to say the least undisciplined student, who could hardly endure the authority of teachers whom he did not like and who felt exactly the same about him. Bad at languages, hardly gifted for the arts or literature, a declared enemy of dancing and social life, he had good grades in mathematics only.

In the winter of 1783, the famous improvised episode of the snowball battle took place in the school courtyard. That moral success was however short-lived, and he decided to devote himself to studying French in order to put an end to the constant mockery he was the target of. Thirty years later however, with the Empire in its last days, he would continue to use sometimes peculiar expressions which would betray his corsican origins.

The student-officer was happy to see again, in the summer of 1784, his father who was then visiting the region. His mother had visited him two years earlier: "She was so shocked by my thinness and the modification of my features that she claimed that they had changed me and hesitated before recognizing me. I had, indeed, changed a great deal because I was working during recreation time... It was not in my nature to accept the idea of not being the best in my class."

Napoleon was now fifteen years old. He was preparing the entrance examination to the Ecole Militaire

of Paris. Camp marshal Chevalier de Keralio, a former school inspector at Brienne, wrote in a report which, in hindsight, lacked perceptiveness:

"Good constitution, excellent health, obedient character, honest and grateful. His behavior is very regular. He always excelled in the study of mathematics. He knows history and geography tolerably well. He has very poor social skills."

His conclusion is indeed rather amazing when we know what followed: "*He will make an excellent sailor.*"

The official school inspector, Reynaud des Monts, interviewed the student Buonaparte at the end of September and declared him fit for the Ecole Militaire. On October 17, 1784, the future "sailor" left Brienne with four of his classmates. A few days later, they reached the capital.

In Paris

The first contact with the school was unpleasant: the non-commissioned officers assigned to supervise the newcomers were "giving orders in a commanding military tone," something however hardly surprising in an institution training future officers… But Napoleon Buonaparte, with his rebellious spirit and corsican temperament, could hardly stand to be given orders and was not very enthusiastic either about handling weapons. One day, when the "elder" directing the drill gave him a rap on the knuckles as a call to order, the young Corsican threw his rifle at him and asserted that he would take no more criticism from him.

Bad at drill exercises, next to last in mathematics, which were his forte, Buonaparte was not giving much satisfaction to his new teachers. They showed however

The mythical snowball fight at the academy of Brienne

It was in the particularly harsh winter of 1783 that the famous scene, where the young warrior would show his exceptional gifts for strategy, took place. All witnesses agree in their description of an impetuous, soon to be domineering Buonaparte.
Horace Vernet (1789-1863), dated 1822.

infinite patience with him, entrusting him to the care of one of his schoolmates, Alexandre des Mazis, in order to tame him, and incorporating him in the battalion in spite of his ignorance of the manoeuvres to perform. The command "Order… arms!", dear to all the armies in the world, was leaving the adolescent dreamy, so dreamy indeed that he was forgetting the order and was the only one remaining with his rifle in the air, much to the despair of the commander, who was begging:

"Monsieur Buonaparte, wake up! You always make us miss the beat of the drill!"

But Monsieur Buonaparte dreaded to wake up: he was dreaming of Corsica which he had not seen for more than six years. His teachers would have been undoubtedly in favor of his return there: he was reading history books in German class, was expelled from the writing class, was discouraging his literature professor who had given up trying to read his spidery scrawl, was bickering with his geography and history teacher over Corsica… Fencing was one of his great passions, but he took to it with a passion absolutely devoid of method, uttering wild screams without protecting himself from his opponents' blows and breaking many a foil. When the exercise was over, Napoleon seemed like *"a small, dark young man, sad, gloomy, stern yet argumentative and a great talker."* During this period, his conversations were often centered on the same preoccupations: to rant and rave against the "torturers" of his native land and to curse with increasing exasperation those who supported it.

The examination open to all the royal military schools took place in September 1785. Napoleon passed 42nd out of the 58 admitted. One of the examiners wrote down his impressions: *"Reserved and hard working, prefers studying to any kind of amusement, enjoys reading good authors; very keen on abstract sciences, little curiosity for the others; knows thoroughly mathematics and geography; quiet, preferring solitude, temperamental and haughty, extremely prone to selfishness, does not talk much, scathing at repartee, very proud, ambitious and aspiring to everything; this young man deserves our protection."*

In the fall of 1785, Napoleon Buonaparte left the Ecole Militaire of Paris to everyone's satisfaction. He himself had nothing to complain about: he was promoted to second lieutenant and assigned to the regiment of La Fère in Valence. It was for him the beginning of a new life.

Garrison life

Charles Buonaparte had died in Montpellier in February 1785. His death increased the family responsibilities of the adolescent who, although he was not the eldest, was showing more character than his brother Joseph. His promotion to the rank of artillery officer (there were no openings in the navy that year) gave him the opportunity to finish his studies, to finally earn a living and to send money to his mother. For the young Corsican so eager to have his worth recognized, the main thing was that he had become *something*, if not *someone* yet.

"I was an officer at the age of sixteen years and fifteen days," he would write later in the memories of his youth. That simple statement can hardly hide the tremendous pride felt by the Emperor on receiving his first commission.

Billeted on Mademoiselle Bou in town, the little lieutenant was then enjoying a pleasant life between his light duties, meals with his friends, balls, trips to the Dauphiné countryside, and a few parties organised by the city's "high" society. This is how he became friendly with a Madame du Colombier and especially with her daughter, Mademoiselle Caroline, with whom he would go and pick cherries… in all innocence. In the secret of his room, he was also devoting a great deal of time to writing and reading. His diverse and wide-ranging reading would give him a considerable advantage a few years later when his prodigious imagination, fed by his legal and historical, geographical and philosophic knowledge, would put him far above his rivals for power. Books would give him a depth and strength of vision, sometimes prophetic, which would surpass his contemporaries' ones. Because of the times, he became passionate about Rousseau and the *Social Contract*... All that would change.

He bravely undertook to write a *History of Corsica*, which was from then on magnified in his mind by all the ideal representations of the island made by his favorite authors. He also wrote a ranting invocation to the heroes of corsican freedom. Another time, it was a romantic meditation: *"Always alone among others, I return home to dream with myself and to surrender to my intense melancholy. Which side is it leaning towards today? Towards death…"*

He actually did not think only of his own death:

"If I had only one man to destroy in order to free my compatriots, I would leave at once and I would plunge my sword into the tyrant's heart to avenge my homeland and the laws he violated…"

He was still pursuing his Corsican dream: second lieutenant Buonaparte, who so proudly sported the uniform of His Majesty's artillery, needed only a riot and the reappearance of Paoli to turn at once into one of the most ardent corsican patriots. He was haunted by his island that was distorted by so many years of absence and so much personal misery.

The time was nearing however when he would be able to see it again: in August 1786, judging that his first six months of service justified a short rest, he received his semi-annual leave. Unable to contain his joy, he hurried on his way back comparing Corsica to the Promised Land… But he wrote beforehand, doubtful and suddenly worried:

"What shall I see in my country? My fellow countrymen bound in chains and trembling as they kiss the hand that oppresses them?"

In fact, the return to Corsica was very disappointing for the young exile. He happily met up again with his family, which had in the meantime expanded with brothers and sisters born while he was away, but immediately had to defend their financial interests, as the family was crippled with debts since Charles Buonaparte's death. He also rediscovered his country with a youthful enthusiasm which quickly cooled down:

"From then on, I started to wonder about the love of freedom I thought all Corsicans nurtured in their hearts."

His strides in the bush along with local peasants and his discussions with them profoundly disappointed him. Where was the flame of heroic times? Where were the brave men whom for so long he thought of leading against the abhorred French? He found the people lukewarm and resigned to the "foreign occupation," smiling at his impassioned speeches as adults might smile at the prattle of a foolish child. And the country seemed so poor compared to the opulent cities of France! To console himself for this setback, Napoleon continued to read assiduously: Rousseau of course (had he not sung the praise of Corsica?), but also Montesquieu, Tacitus, Montaigne, Titus Lavinius, Racine, Plato and a few others.

Thanks to a first extension of his leave in April 1787, family affairs becoming really worrying, lieutenant Buonaparte could make a trip to Paris in the fall to enable him to refer his various claims to the very headquarters of the administrative departments involved. This stay also allowed him to idle away his time in the capital, and particularly in the neighbourhood of the Palais-Royal, where a streetwalker invited him to do a lot more than pick cherries…

During a brief return to Corsica in May 1788, following another extension of leave which he obtained in December 1787 *"to regain his health,"* he managed to express his convictions on independence to two young officers of his regiment who judged him to be *"curt and sententious for a young man his age."*

Napoleon had at long last to decide to rejoin his corps in Auxonne: he had indeed left it twenty-one months ago. These were trying times for the young officer who was striving to save some money from his pay to send it back to his family. He was living frugally, was turning ill-tempered and hardly amiable, and was ready to fight a duel for even the slightest cause. He was more especially exasperated by his neighbour who had developed a "malicious taste" for blowing a horn. They nearly came to blows, but a council of their peers helped with a compromise: *"One will play the horn farther away, and the other will be more tolerant."*

The cause of his bitterness? A deep despair, certainly. What was left of his past dreams? Corsica, under the yoke of the French "occupying forces," had bitterly betrayed his expectations; his future was all mapped out, he would have to serve *ad vitam aeternam* a nation he professed to hate —*"the most hideous people on earth"*— without any hope of promotion to higher ranks, due to his "minor" nobility.

On the first of January 1789, his housekeeper, filled with good resolutions, wished him to be one day a general… He sighed, letting the injury heal a little, and murmured sadly:

"General? General! Ah, my poor Thérèse, I would be all too satisfied if I could be promoted to the rank of commander. I would not ask for more…"

That was a few months before the beginning of the French Revolution.

THE SOLDIER OF FORTUNE
1789-1804

An Adventurer in the Revolution: 1789-1796

The corsican Patriot: 1789-1793

The Great Hope: 1789-1791

"Equality, which was to help work my way up, did appeal to me," the Emperor would say later, when remembering the days of 1789. However, that appeal seems indeed retrospective, if we look in detail at his schedule at the time.

In April, second lieutenant Buonaparte is said to have had monks from the Cîteaux abbey arrested for sedition (they wanted to drink the wine from their vineyards rather than to sell it) on his own initiative. He was first and foremost a soldier whose duty was to maintain order against the "rabble," ready to fire at the crowd if he were given the order to do so. New ideas were attractive to him, but they remained just theories when chaos was directly at hand. He started to think about how he could turn to his advantage the situation which was worsening a little more every day and the unrest which appeared increasingly to be getting out of hand.

Quick to think and act, the young Napoleon felt that the time would come soon to accomplish great things in his native Corsica. His hopes went quite naturally to Paoli, the old exile in England. Mid-June, the low-ranking officer summoned up his courage to write his hero a very elaborate letter which would remain unanswered. The letter began in unequivocal terms: *"I was born when the Fatherland was perishing [...] The cries of the dying, the groans of the oppressed, the tears of despair surrounded my cradle ever since I was born..."*

After July 14, upon receiving news from Paris and hearing of the fall of the Bastille, he announced that he was *"extremely alarmed."* But was he worried then about the future of France? No, only Corsica interested him. He was viewing the consequences of events only from the perspective of his "patriotic" interests. Seeing things rapidly evolve (abolition of Privileges and Declaration of Human Rights during the night of August 4), he asked for another leave from August 9. He was given that leave he was entitled to without delay. He landed in Corsica in September, happy to finally see the conditions favorable to his projects. The worries of the Crown, while weakening the French authority, worked to his advantage. That was what he noticed initially: "Equality" would come much later, when he would be above all the others.

When Napoleon Buonaparte landed in Ajaccio at the end of September 1789, he was twenty years old and thought he had lived only for that moment. The whole island was in turmoil; opinions were divided into three main trends: the royalist party, the nationalist party calling for the return of Paoli and the people's party, soon to become the republican one, headed by the lawyer Salicetti.

Salicetti felt that Corsica should be integrated into the "new France" to benefit from the Revolution then underway. Second lieutenant Buonaparte supported the republicans despite his veneration for Paoli, aware of the need to forge an alliance with the revolutionaries —even if they were French— to defeat the counter-revolution which remained powerful on the island. Corsican people were apathetic and the masses seemed indifferent to the events in France: in spite of

The meeting between Buonaparte and Paoli in July 1790

Paoli's stand had at first inspired the young Buonaparte and had given him political reasons to hate France. But the revolutionary activist met a worn hero, who felt only contempt for the "little scheming lieutenant." His unshakeable faith in Paoli would be affected forever. He started to imagine a more solitary destiny.

27

the political agitation fanned by the different opposing parties, the royal flag was still flying over the whole island as if nothing were happening.

As for the commander in chief of the royal troops, a certain viscount de Sarrin, he only wanted to "hold" his fortresses, and to try to calm down the most hot-headed people with patience and diplomacy. This wise policy prevented a confrontation, but could not be followed for long without risk. Already Salicetti and his followers had demanded the formation of a National Guard, a project rejected by Sarrin and the royalist nobility.

It was in this confused situation that Napoleon decided to play the role he had been preparing himself for so long. His military training was prompting him to try and take command of the communal militia, while his brother Joseph, secretary of the "Ajaccio Committee of the 36," wanted to be a member of the legislative assembly.

Their most important rivals were Pozzo di Borgo and Peraldi, who were particularly strong in the region around Bastia, and much more renowned and powerful overall. Napoleon and his brother would make up for their lack of political recognition (the example of their father's "treason" must have significantly lessened the impact of their impassionate speeches) with a tremendous activity. The second lieutenant of his Majesty's army was writing epistles to the National Assembly, was militating against the supporters of the Ancien Régime, was happily spending a lot of energy while being carried away by the course of events and the thought of flirting with history, if only during a speech or a meeting with "patriots." Joseph stood for election and became president of the Directorate of Ajaccio in October.

On November 5, the municipal officers of Bastia finally created a National Guard despite Sarrin's opposition; the troops fired at the crowd who looted the citadel and seized 1200 muskets. The future Emperor made himself so well noticed by the side of the rioters that viscount de Sarrin personally asked him to return to Ajaccio. On December 26, the commander of Ajaccio wrote to the Minister of War saying that it would be better to reassign second lieutenant Buonaparte to his regiment, *"because he constantly foments unrest."*

Although Napoleon Buonaparte had looked like an "activist" during these first few months of the Revolution, he still appeared in fact awkward and without any real influence on the course of events. But he got to know men and the inner workings of politics, an essential experience for the future head of state. The care he later took to rely on an effective police force shows how much he remembered the part it played then, and knew the importance of a police organization able to foresee and put down these kinds of popular turmoil... The decree incorporating Corsica into France was promulgated in January 1790: the island of Beauty ceased to be considered, legally at least, as a conquered land and became French territory. The news was greeted with real enthusiasm, and Napoleon, who less than a year earlier would have unscrupulously massacred Frenchmen, declared with the same strong conviction to Abbé Reynal:

"From now on, we have the same interests, the same concerns, the sea no longer separates us."

Was this the same man to express himself in this way? Certainly not, this was a man who, going back to Corsica shaped by ideals, had sacrificed them to political realism without hesitation. Corsica could not be independent? So be it, there was the French side to be played, a decision which allowed him to keep his position of officer of the royal army. Presented with a cruel dilemma by the Revolution, Napoleon opted for a quest for power (or for a role to play) by conveniently "forgetting" his former hatred. But, out of convenience only: he will still often denounce *"those base souls who were the first to throw themselves into the French's arms..."*

Another event undoubtedly led him in the same direction: his meeting with Paoli at Ponte Nuovo in July 1790. The great corsican leader had returned from exile, but no longer fitted the idealized childhood image that Napoleon had fancied. The hero of independence, whose mind and body had thickened, was indeed showing little support for the Revolution and no specific fondness for the Buonaparte clan. The one whom he would contemptuously call the "little scheming lieutenant" would still remain for some time one of his most faithful followers, but there was now a slight gap between them that would lead the young man to another dilemma: to continue to serve Paoli... or to serve Napoleon Buonaparte...

1792: Buonaparte in the uniform of lieutenant-colonel of the 1ˢᵗ Battalion of Corsica

Thanks to an inheritance expected from his uncle, Napoleon invested financially in politics. He got the rank of lieutenant-colonel in the Corsican National Guard, a significant success that spared him the obligation to rejoin his corps. But his ambiguous conduct during the riots in Ajaccio forced him to leave Corsica for a while, which gave him the opportunity to witness the storming of the Tuileries.
Henri-Félix-Emmanuel Philippoteaux (1815-1884), dated 1834.
Musée du château de Versailles.

The end of a dream: 1791-1793

Compelled to rejoin his regiment in Auxonne in February 1791, Napoleon spent there several feverish months. He was deeply tormented by his idleness and his being away from the unfolding drama he felt he had a role to play in. He killed his impatience by reworking his *History of Corsica*. Sounded out about writing the preface for The Work, Paoli answered with contempt that *"history cannot written in the years of youth."* This double meaning sentence added even more uneasiness between the young officer (now a first lieutenant) and his former role model.

After having visited General du Teil, his protector, who had singled him out during his latest "stay" in France, lieutenant Buonaparte managed to secure another special leave of several months for the elections of the legislative Assembly which were to take place in Corte at the end of September 1791.

The inheritance from their uncle, the Archdeacon Lucien, came just at the right moment and allowed the Buonaparte brothers to financially invest in politics. The funds they lacked the year before now served them well: although Joseph did not succeed in being elected deputy, Napoleon won (with the help of a little incentive to one of the commissioners) the rank of lieutenant-colonel in the Corsican National Guard. This was an important success which spared him the obligation to rejoin his regiment: he did not know however how to make good use of that success, and spent his time and energy in skirmishes and inconsequential fights. The eagle had not flown the nest yet.

His ambiguous conduct during the riots in Ajaccio had created suspicion and he was forced to leave Corsica for a while. After an altercation between some sailors and his men, he had tried to seize illegally the citadel of Ajaccio, but its commander had successfully refused. At the end of May 1782, he went to Paris to witness some historic events: on June 20, the people humiliated the King, on August 10, an angry mob massacred the Swiss Guards during the storming of the Tuileries. The Monarchy was abolished.

First Lieutenant Buonaparte was then just commenting on the events, calling Louis XVI corsican names and denouncing his weakness that was preventing him from shelling the rioters. *"If I were the king, it would not have happened that way,"* he asserted on June 20, at the Tuileries.

His main worry however was to be reinstated in the army which had reported him a deserter. The war which had just been declared between revolutionary France and the German Holy Roman Empire did make matters easier: the "Fatherland in danger" could not in fact do without young officers whose training had been so costly to the Ancien Régime. Even better, he was promoted to the rank of captain! But he was indeed aware that his "genius" had nothing to do with it.

He would write to his family:

"You know as well as I do that I am a captain only because all the field officers from the regiment of La Fère are in Coblenz."

That is in the ranks of the exiles.

The fall of the Monarchy made calling for a Convention necessary. Napoleon decided to return to Corsica to shoot his bolt: Joseph had to be elected deputy and he himself had to get back into his fellow countrymen's favour… whether they like it or not.

To regain his prestige which suffered so much from the Ajaccio affair, Napoleon volunteered to participate in an attack aimed against Sardinia. The operations, carried out in January and February 1793, failed. The situation became untenable for the Buonapartes who had not reached enough recognition to play a prominent role in Corsica. The strongest party was headed by the ageing Paoli who had become increasingly conservative over the years, and was turning away from the revolution. He even considered giving the island of Beauty to England, as he could not guarantee its independence.

This time the gap was too wide to be filled; for the past three years Napoleon had been walking a tightrope between French reason and Corsican passion. He did not want to hear a word about England, which would hand over victory to Paoli and eliminate forever his adversaries. A first assassination attempt aimed at the young patriot did not open his eyes. Chased through the streets of Ajaccio by Paoli's partisans, he found refuge in Bastia where he gathered some men to "recapture" his native city.

The civil war which may have resulted from this confrontation (and triggered an English intervention) did not take place however.

August 10, 1792: Buonaparte witnesses the storming of the Tuileries

Buonaparte could assess the weak character of the king when the Swiss Guard was massacred. Louis XVI's hesitation during these decisive hours taught Napoleon how to quell a riot: with cannons. These moments of power vacuum made a lasting impression on his military education.
Nicolas-Toussaint Charlet (1782-1845).
Imp Bertauts, rue Cadet, 11, Paris.
Alliance des Arts.
Marchant Editr.

Cannon fire and a definitely hostile population greeted their landing in Ajaccio. So complete was the defeat that the whole Buonaparte family, led by Madame Laetitia, had to re-embark and escape to the continent.

"This country is not for us," Napoleon told his mother.

He was thus implicitly acknowledging the complete failure of his first political manoeuvres, the only ones inspired by the dreams of his youth. Landing in Toulon on June 13, 1793, with his family, captain Buonaparte was a 24 year-old man events had made precociously mature. At least he understood by then that one does not need ideals to succeed in politics.

For the next few years Napoleon would be the man of the Revolution… or rather, the man of his masters, Robespierre then Barras. He was ready to spring into action at the first given opportunity.

The young general: 1793-1796

In the service of Robespierre: 1793-1794

Napoleon's first campaign was the failed one against Sardinia. He saw there the first signs of his genuine talent, the one he had been searching for since his graduating from military school. It was the sword, not the pen or the word, the usual weapons of those destined for politics.

It was the right time. Great Britain, after long years of neutrality, even benevolence towards the Revolution, has decided not to tolerate French intrusion into Holland and to go to war against the troublemaker. Saved at Valmy by Dumouriez, who after Jemmappes had conquered Belgium, revolutionary France was showing its intentions to "regenerate" all its neighbours and then "free" them from the "tyrants" who oppressed them. War was eagerly sought by the people, as well as by the government which preferred to send its sans-culottes on the rampage on foreign soil. Had not Maret, a member of the French Embassy in London, confided to Pitt, some time before: *"Peace is impossible. We have 300,000 armed men whom we must keep marching as far as their legs will carry them… otherwise, they would retrace their steps and slit our throats."*

A letter from Buonaparte to General Carteaux: the siege of Toulon, 1793

In Corsica, Napoleon had not found favorable conditions for his potential leadership to blossom. In Toulon, he showed Barras that he could depend on him in the future.
Musée de Brienne.

The various episodes of the Belgian campaign had not inordinately moved captain Buonaparte, who was then being chased out of Corsica. That did not stop him, once "converted" to the French cause by the turn of events, to tell those he sought the protection of:

"I sacrificed my native land. I abandoned my possessions. I lost everything for the Republic…"

He also wrote a pamphlet, The Supper at Beaucaire, to dispel the sceptics' last doubts:

"Can one be revolutionary enough? Marat and Robespierre, here are my saints!"

Those would disappoint him less than Paoli, but he would realize later that pantheon was not eternal.

Moved by such patriotic devotion, his protectors did not need a lot of persuasion: after a mission in Avignon, he had the good fortune to meet Salicetti who offered him the position of commander of the artillery of the army of General Carteaux, a former house painter who had also been an occasional gendarme, an utterly incompetent soldier but a spruce one, *"from head to toe,"* in his uniform.

The good fortune of Buonaparte at this time was to be a trained officer in an army of which most officers had gone into exile. Although he had not become indispensable yet, the military were happy to find him at a moment's notice to replace battalion leader Dommartin, who had been wounded at Ollioules.

The army was advancing on Toulon, which had declared itself against the Republic by welcoming the English, who, making the most of that opportunity, had brought in troops; their ships were occupying the bay and defending with their cannons the access to the city. Carteaux and his staff imagined bombarding them by firing at will. This master plan was delayed however on the advice of the young captain of artillery, who recommended to make *"a trial run to gauge the range before firing at will."*

The test was convincing, demonstrating to an astonished Carteaux that the range was only one third of the distance.

Napoleon Buonaparte sensed then that there was something to be achieved in Toulon. He had the stage he lacked in Corsica, with an ideal audience, among which Viscount Paul de Barras who had been put in

au général Carteaux

L'on travaille archenne; mais les hommes
sont fatigués. veuillez, donner l'ordre aux
400 hommes pour travailler — les rhos till point le

Le Commandant de la [...]
Bonaparte

Viscount Paul de Barras, the man behind Bonaparte's success.

On St Helena, Napoleon remembered Barras in this way: "He was a very poor speaker and he was not in the habit of working [...] During the crisis of Thermidor 9, the Convention designated him to march against the Commune which had risen up in support of Robespierre; and he won. That event brought him fame. [...] On 12 Vendémiaire, [...] circumstances were too serious for him; they were beyond his capacities. It was not Barras who made the war." According to Napoleon, the Convention would have failed without Bonaparte. How to turn political ingratitude into an art!

E. RONIAT

charge of supervising the operation by the Convention. Barras quickly noticed the young Corsican who, from then on, became one of his followers, and courted Napoleon with the same ardour he was expending on seducing General Carteaux's wife.

Sensing the eye of destiny (as well as Barras' one) on him, Napoleon was everywhere at once, just as he had been during the first months of the Revolution in Corsica: he was ubiquitous, fearless, wounded several times, tireless, farsighted, knowing how to make himself appreciated and placing his extensive knowledge in the service of his cause. The expected result was not long in coming: Barras grew to appreciate the inventor of the "Battery of Fearless Men," and recognized him as an officer of great talent. Having both ambition and common sense, the future Director decided to favor his new protégé, who might be useful to him one day.

Carteaux was dismissed and finally replaced by General Dugommier who quickly understood the situation, referring to Buonaparte as *"your little protégé"* when speaking to Barras. Napoleon was gaining importance, was submitting a plan of attack that was accepted and was rising in rank rapidly. He arrived in Toulon in September 1793, was made a battalion leader on October 18, then an adjutant-general on December 1, and finally a brigadier general on December 22, when he was 24 years old, a few days after the English withdrawal from the city.

Promoted commander of the artillery of the army of Italy in February 1784, the new general was able to enjoy a few months of rest. While inspecting the coastline, he made friends with Augustin de Robespierre, who was far less "incorruptible" than his brother Maximilien.

At least in the beginning, this connection helped him beyond all expectations. The good Augustin would write to Paris that *"citizen Buonaparte, the artillery commander, is of transcendent merit."*

It was then, when everything was going right that Napoleon became enthusiastic about conquering Italy. He was made optimistic by the benevolence of his high-ranking protectors and he began thinking about a campaign strategy to seize the peninsula. He would carry out successfully, two years later, that same plan, reworked and adapted.

While waiting for this big event, time was spent on the "preparatory operations," the plans of which were sent for approval to the Committee for Public Safety, always through the intermediary of Augustin de Robespierre. These projects were entirely dictated by general Buonaparte to Lieutenant Junot, his aide-de-camp, whom he had met in Toulon.

One event, however, would stop his dazzling rise to success: the fall of Robespierre. His followers were unmercifully tracked down and promptly eliminated from key offices. On August 7, two days before his arrest, the future Emperor still had time to write a proclamation of faith in the Republic:

"I was rather affected by Robespierre's catastrophe, a man I liked and believed honest, but even if he had been my brother, I would have stabbed him to death myself, had he aspired to tyranny..."

Napoleon, who thought then that he was "finished," was finally set free without being officially reinstated in his command. But there was such a need for his knowledge and inspiration to drive back the Piedmontese counter-offensive that a gout-ridden General Dumerbion, commander in chief of the Army of Italy, humbly asked him: *"My child, give me a plan as you know how to make them, and I shall carry it out as best I can."* Apart from his recognized talents as a strategist and his rank of general of artillery, which was detrimental to him because it was due to Robespierre's good offices, his situation was much the same as when he had arrived from Corsica.

He had to start everything all over again.

In the service of Barras: 1794-1796

The end of the year 1794 was gloomy and 1795 started badly: Napoleon was crossed off the artillery lists where there were too many generals, and transferred to the infantry. Even worse, the military thought of sending him to Vendée, whereas he was fully devoting himself to organizing an expedition to "free" Corsica from the English who had been welcomed by Paoli. But the British fleet had been on the lookout and managed to destroy the French vessels, and with them his last hopes.

At the same time, General Scherer petitioned Paris to get rid of the Corsican officers who were a burden to him and *"whose patriotism was more dubious than their disposition to grow rich."* Vendée did not attract at all General Buonaparte, who considered he had nothing to gain by fighting on a secondary and ungratifying front. He much preferred to remain at the disposal of the Army of Italy, keeping one eye on the Alps and the other on Corsica.

On May 8, 1795, along with his faithful Junot, his brother Louis and Marmont, Napoleon set off for Paris with the aim of convincing the headquarters' staff that he was really not made to brave the weather of Vendée. He was leaving behind, in tears, a certain Désirée Clary whom he had been recently engaged to, and who would reign one day over Sweden at Bernadotte's side.

On the way to the capital, he made the acquaintance of Madame de Chastenay to whom he casually confided:

"Happiness, for a man, must consist in stretching his aptitudes to their limits."

He would spend a lot of energy in the following months to be able to be happy. His confidant, who was very perceptive, wrote about him: *"I think that Buonaparte would have emigrated, had emigration offered him opportunities for success."* It mattered little which cause Napoleon served! Sooner or later it would become his own.

The fiery reputation of his former protégé made Viscount de Barras, who was ruling in Paris, cautious. As they had many enemies, he was able to spare him temporarily Vendée, but could not send him back to the Army of Italy. His ambitions crushed, depressed, broke, suffering from a new chill in his relationship with Désirée Clary, contemplating suicide, Napoleon wandered the streets of Paris a tortured soul. He sadly confided to his brother Joseph that *"life meant so little,"* and that *"if it goes on like this, my friend, I shall end by not getting out of the way of a passing carriage."*

Returning to some of his old demons, he wrote too a novel, Clisson and Eugénie, in which he presented the story of his love affair with Désirée, and related his disappointments and his despair at being treated cruelly by fate. The work ends with a few phrases in a tragic style, betraying his state of mind at that time:

Clisson to Eugénie (or Napoleon to Désirée, or Napoleon to Fate...):

"May you live happily without thinking anymore of unhappy Clisson! Kiss my sons! Let them not have the passionate soul of their father; they would be like him the victims of other men, of glory and love..."

When the "victim" was not chafing at the bit, he was preparing his plan for the invasion of Italy with all the more care as he had time.

He reached a low point on August 16, upon receiving his marching orders to Vendée. Determined to be finished with it, he appeared before the Committee of Public Safety to play his last cards and detail his campaign plan for Italy. Doulcet de Pontécoulant, the new Minister of War, listened and encouraged him to develop his theory. He was asked to write a letter to Kellerman, then commander in chief of the Army of Italy. The Emperor would smile when remembering that time:

"I wrote the letter and reprimanded Kellerman for the errors he had made and the course of action he was recommending, and delineated the position he should have taken. As the letter was to be signed by the president of the Committee, I used the tone I would use today, which the Committee did enjoy."

It worked, and the young strategist did not have to go to Vendée; he had however to stay in Paris where he was immediately assigned to the topographical office of the Committee for Public Safety. As he had no bureaucratic soul, it was not long before he became exceedingly bored and thought for a moment about leaving for Constantinople, while a paternal Barras was urging patience.

Paris experienced both celebrations and famine in the summer of 1795. That paradoxical situation was encouraging conspirators of all sorts to plot against the government, which was adroitly treading a delicate course, lashing out at all sides while remaining overall threatening. The people, who were starving, were infuriated by what had become of their Revolution;

The attack of Saint-Roch church by Buonaparte on 13 Vendémiaire Year IV (October 5, 1795).

The deciding episode of the day unfolds there: Parisian National Guards, who had been drawn into a rebellion inspired by the constitutional monarchy, had assembled on the steps of Saint-Roch church. They planned to make their way to the Tuileries palace by way of the Dauphin cul-de-sac, almost opposite it. They were stopped by the "Patriots of 1789" who used the artillery Buonaparte had installed there. The frightening efficiency of his men's fire would earn him the nickname of "general Vendémiaire."

and monarchist circles were more than happy to fan their discontent. The "Thermidorians," led by Barras, did enjoy their power while keeping at the same time an eye on the streets.

A chance event would soon set off this powder keg. The decrees of August 1795, which dissolved the Convention and created the Directory, also provided for the creation of two councils, the Council of Five Hundred and the Council of Elders. But the

Conventionnels, careful not to lose their advantages while pushing aside the "Monarchiens" and the "Feuillants," had stipulated that two-thirds of the newly elected delegates should come from their assembly. In the morning of October 4, the two sections most opposed to the Convention, the Le Peletier and Théâtre-Français (Odéon) ones, sent out a proclamation announcing that the *"drinkers of blood have just been handed weapons at the Tuileries."*

The royalist factions, which were waiting for the right moment, rose up in mass. Appointed commander in chief of the army of the Interior and given the responsibility to put down the revolt, Barras brought in his protégé as second-in-command. For Buonaparte, his time had come to become "general Vendémiaire."

"I value the title of general Vendémiaire, he will say one day. *It will be, in the future, my first title of glory…"*

For the moment being, it was simply a question of using cannons against the insurgents: who better than an artillery officer could do the job?

Until that time, cannons had only been used as supporting weapons: but Napoleon's training allowed him to put them to a better use. Learning that forty cannons were being stored at the Sablons plains, a fast thinking and imperious Napoleon Buonaparte gave orders to a young cavalry officer by the name of Joachim Murat:

"Take two hundred horses, go immediately to the Sablons plains and bring back the guns and equipment. Make sure to find them. Hack your way through, if need be. I hold you accountable for it. Now leave!"

Murat's swift execution of these orders would determine the day's outcome. Barras and Napoleon organized the defense of the Tuileries, benefiting from the lessons learnt from the unfortunate experience of Louis XVI in 1792. The fate of the royal uprising was decided around four-thirty in the afternoon. The first shot was fired in front of Saint-Roch church. No one knows which side started it, the royalist factions or the "patriots of 89" who were defending the Tuileries. In any case, the shot was the signal for the street battle.

Bonaparte's cannons enfiladed the Dauphin cul-de-sac which led to Saint-Roch church. The insurgents had concentrated in this sector in preparation for an attack on the Tuileries. Bonaparte brought forward a cannon *"the shot of which served as a signal for all the posts,"* he will acknowledge in his Mémorial. The first shots were made with grapeshot or cannonballs as a show of strength.

The clash lasted only a short time, and Barras' forces were soon able to "mop up" the neighbouring streets. At four o'clock in the morning, Saint-Roch church, abandoned by its defenders, was retaken without a fight.

What was the final toll of human losses during these events? We can assume that Napoleon in St Helena kept rather close to reality when he gave a figure of two hundred killed or wounded for the "sectionnaires" and nearly as many for the defenders of the Convention, with most of the latter killed in front of Saint-Roch church at the outset of the battle.

The confrontation ended in favour of Barras, mainly due to the talents of his young protégé. On October 5, the royalist party was silenced then for what would last a long time. Barras, about to become a Director himself, one of the five "kings" of France under the Directory, thanked Napoleon by appointing him to his former position of commander in chief of the army of the Interior. It is then that, frenchifying his name, Buonaparte became Bonaparte.

The success of the young general was spectacular, but he was still not happy. Something remained unaccomplished in him, which made him view his command of the army of the Interior as a temporary position. There was only one army in the world that could satisfy the ambitions of Napoleon at that time: the army of Italy.

A future empress entered then the scene: Joséphine de Beauharnais, née Marie-Josèphe Rose Tascher de La Pagerie, a beautiful Creole with a fiery temperament, an expert in courtly love, a former mistress of Barras who belonged to the Faubourg Saint-Germain high society.

Although he was interested in the woman's assumed wealth (two millions avowed, but much more in undisclosed debts), Napoleon remained a little doubtful. His fervent desire to marry was known to everyone, but was she the ideal choice? Barras and Madame Tallien were convinced that she was the one. On October 28, 1795, to entice him into an arrangement, Joséphine herself wrote to him, as encouraging as she could be to this still unknown, and not very talkative general with a bilious complexion:

"You no longer come to see a friend who is fond of you... You are wrong because she is tenderly attached to you... Come to lunch with me tomorrow. I need to see you and chat with you about your interests."

That "chat" was apparently captivating: Napoleon went back every night for five months, until they were married. The excellent Barras, no doubt a little dishonest and debauched, but of a basically good character, gave the army of Italy as a wedding present. The main mission of the twenty-six year old commander in chief, should he conquer Italy, was to plunder the country so as to line coffers (and pockets) then desperately empty.

The epic was about to begin.

39

The apprenticeship of Power: 1796-1804

The beginnings of an epic: 1796-1799

The Campaign of Italy: 1796-1797

The campaign of Italy so marks the beginnings of the Napoleonic epic that the Emperor in 1813 would use the phrase *"putting on his Italian boots"* to revive his reputation as a great strategist. It is in northern Italy that the extraordinary destiny of the little Corsican, eager to succeed, would take shape.

His arrival in Nice on March 27, 1796, had however been coolly welcomed by an army that considered him, not without cause, as a bedroom general. The generals in the division, the irreplaceable Berthier, Masséna (who considered him a schemer and an idiot), Serurier, Augereau (who called him an imbecile), Laharpe, found it difficult not to show their condescension towards this puny, sallow little fellow who intended to lead them to battle.

Their opinions would quickly change; even if they did not like him more, they learnt to respect him. Because Napoleon knew how to speak to his men.

"As soon as he arrived, Bonaparte's attitude was one of a man born to rule" wrote Marmont. Awkward in drawing rooms, a provincial with the "grand lady" Joséphine he had chosen for his wife, the young general felt in his element at the head of this army he dreamed of for so long.

The army of Italy looked however a sorry sight. Suffering from the negligence of the government and the incompetence of the administration, it was poorly equipped, dressed in rags and had not been paid in months. Salicetti had however been sent to prepare it for the forthcoming campaign, and material conditions were improving from day to day. As for its morale, it must have been sharply boosted by the replacement of the shy Scherer by a young general with a strong personality, clearly ambitious but determined to go on the offensive.

That offensive went down in history, lightning and fatal for the king of Sardinia who, after less than a month of battle, was forced to call an armistice. The Piedmont representatives sent to haggle over the terms of the treaty discovered, at their expense, that General Bonaparte was no diplomat:

"I might lose battles, but you will never see me waste time out of confidence or laziness!"

Once the Piedmont lock burst open, the army could enter the Po Valley held by the Austrians. On May 10, at the bridge of Lodi, Napoleon drove them out of Lombardy to everyone's surprise, before entering Milan as a liberator. The Dukes of Parma and Modena did not waste time suing for peace, which was signed in exchange of heavy war indemnities... a part of which only made it to Paris.

It was a well-led campaign against disunited enemies, a few of them having been bought through Haller, a shady financier offering nevertheless valuable services. The developments in Italy, a secondary front in comparison to Germany where two armies of 80,000 men were at the same time marching to battle, were all very unexpected. The country, already, was systematically plundered by its liberators who got hold of large numbers of art treasures and of considerable riches.

Bonaparte dates his self-confidence back to that battle which immediately turned to legend. *"It was only on the evening of Lodi,"* he asserts in St Helena *"that I believed I was a superior man and I conceived the ambition of performing great things which hitherto had filled my thoughts only as a fantastic dream."* The report addressed to the Directory betrays that self-confidence:

Headquarters, Lodi, 22 Floréal Year IV
[May 11, 1796]

"As soon as the army arrived, it formed a tight column led by the second battalion of infantry with all the other infantry battalions charging behind, shouting Long Live the Republic!"

Bonaparte on the bridge of Arcola, on November 17, 1796

An Austrian counteroffensive, after Bonaparte's success at Lodi in May the previous year, forced him back into battle: this was the "second" Campaign of Italy, which lasted from August 1796 until September 1797. After serious difficulties, he managed to bring the situation under control, and showed the extent of his military skills at the battle of Arcola. Antoine-Jean Gros (1771-1835), 1796. Musée du château de Versailles.

"When we arrived on the bridge [...] we came under extremely heavy enemy fire [...]. Our formidable column ran over everything in its path [...]. Although since the beginning of the campaign we have had very heated exchanges and the army of the Republic had to take huge risks, none of them comes close to the terrible crossing of the bridge of Lodi."

That total and unexpected success went to the head of the young general who forgot all about the factors which had contributed to his victory: experienced field officers, bribed or mediocre adversaries and friendly populations. He neglected to take into account the terrible losses sustained by the French army. Having fulfilled his Italian dream after having lost his Corsican one, Napoleon felt the urge to launch out into new conquests.

"After Lodi, I no longer considered myself a mere general, but a man called upon to decide the fate of peoples. It occurred to me that I could become a truly important actor on our political scene."

It was a thought shared by the Directors who, astonished by the tone of the reports they were receiving, began to tremble. The Milanese came to know their "liberators;" they rebelled quite quickly but were harshly brought to heel.

"In the final analysis, Napoleon then concludes, *one needs to be a soldier to rule; you tame a horse only with boots and spurs."*

The tone was set, and General Bonaparte was ruling northern Italy from Milan, having gathered a small court around him and dealing with the neighbouring powers (Naples and the Holy See, among others) without much concern for what the Directory could possibly want.

An Austrian counteroffensive prompted the second campaign of Italy which would last from August 1796 until January 1797. After some difficult moments, Napoleon managed to regain the upper hand, demonstrating his real worth as a military leader at the battle of Arcola (November 17, 1796). From then on, it was no longer possible to hold him back. In Vienna, Thugat, the Foreign Secretary, commented in despair, *"When Bonaparte, a twenty-seven year old young man with no experience, and an army, half the strength of our forces, that is nothing more than a pack*

Bonaparte at the Battle of Rivoli, on January 14, 1797
This battle and the fall of Mantua brought Bonaparte unequalled glory. From then on, the Directory, unable to cope, endured the policies of Bonaparte, who behaved like a viceroy in his conquests.
Henri-Félix-Emmanuel Philippoteaux (1815-1884), Salon of 1845.
Musée du château de Versailles.

of brigands and volunteers, can beat all our generals, we are of course led to bemoan our decline and degraded condition."

After the fall of Mantua in January 1797, the glory of Bonaparte, who was brilliantly "supported" by Barras in Paris, was at its height. Unable to cope, the Directory had been reduced to blow on the fire to prevent any backlash against itself. The directives sent to the army of Italy were formulated with a mixture of caution and suspicion: *"It is not, in any way, an order the Directory is giving you, but the expression of its wishes."*

On several occasions when Paris sought to impose its views, Napoleon threatened to *"return to private life,"* which, for a general at that time, meant to go into politics. Worried, Barras and his peers by far preferred to let him rule Italy his way (provided he continued to ship back gold) rather than to see him come back to the capital. He thus annexed Venice and Genoa, and established the Cisalpine Republic in Lombardy on June 29.

A last Austrian counteroffensive led by Archduke Charles ended in disaster, and allowed the French army to advance within one hundred kilometers of Vienna. Emperor Francis II agreed to peace. The negotiations dragged on and on, and led finally to the treaty of Campo-Formio, signed in October 1797. The Directory, which had not been consulted, became infuriated, and decided to order the glorious conqueror back to France.

Thus, in the fall of 1797, Napoleon left Italy for Paris. He had known glory and power in Italy, two things he could no longer do without. He had become aware of his leadership abilities, and was fancying his future as nothing less than to reign supreme.

Having tried and tested his skills in Italy, he was looking for something bigger from then on... A powerful country, for example, with a corrupt and unstable government...

Always talkative, he stated once to two diplomats:

"The nation needs a leader, a leader known for his glory and not by theories the French people will not understand. Let them have rattles, it is enough to make them happy. They will enjoy them, and will thus let themselves be led, as long however as the political agenda is cleverly hidden from them!"

Cleverly!

Napoleon Bonaparte would not be the one to manoeuvre in this second phase of the fulfilment of his political ambitions. He would need a man experienced in the practices and posturings of power, a man to whom intrigue and conspiracy were second nature, an ally who would teach him subtlety and patience: Talleyrand.

General Bonaparte's scarf worn during the Campaign of Egypt

Bonaparte felt his glory was slowly fading in the Parisian drawing rooms. Talleyrand pronounced the magic word: the "Orient." Relieved to see such a cumbersome figure go away, Paris was breathing again. Bonaparte was to follow in Alexander the Great's footsteps. The oriental dream was taking shape.
Musée de La Malmaison.

The mirages of Egypt: 1798-1799

The complicity established between the two men was a political one, immediate and deep; it would last ten years. Back recently from the *"plains of the New World"* where he almost became a trapper, Charles-Maurice de Talleyrand-Périgord had had himself appointed by Barras Foreign Minister of the Directory. Madame de Staël, generous and passionate, had besieged for days the powerful Director before he gave in. Her lover constantly threatened her to run and *"throw himself in the river Seine"* if he were not a minister before long...

The new duties of the former bishop of Autun led him to come into contact with General Bonaparte. On July 26, 1797, Talleyrand wrote his first letter to him, ending it with several sentences worthy of the "great diplomat" he would become:

"I shall hasten to have sent to you the plans the Directory will instruct me to pass on to you, and I shall often been robbed, by fame, your usual spokesman, of the pleasure of reporting how you carried out these plans."

The young master of northern Italy discovered he had a providential ally at the very center of a government which he may have been already considering toppling. They forged close links together when he returned to Paris and they first met, in the morning of December 6, 1797.

Talleyrand orchestrated brilliantly Napoleon's return, lavishing his advice on the 28 year-old conqueror who was not hiding his ambition enough and was doing nothing to charm those who were approaching him. Madame de Staël, soon turned his personal enemy, would judge harshly the victor: *"He held the nation, the votes of which he was seeking, in contempt, and his desire to amaze the human race was void of any enthusiasm..."*

The minister guided his pupil, doing his utmost to present him as less dangerous than he was, and lacing his speeches with praise for the Corsican adventurer's "insatiable love for the fatherland and mankind." He had him elected to the Institut to increase his prestige by having him pass as a scholar.

"*True conquests, the only ones that leave no regret, are those made over ignorance...*" Napoleon stated on that occasion.

But Bonaparte was chafing at the bit, ill at ease in the Parisian drawing rooms where his fame was beginning to fade away. Appointed leader of an army designated to invade England, he had given up that too perilous a plan... when Talleyrand dropped the magic word: the "Orient."

Egypt, to be precise, but why not, too, Syria, Anatolia... Constantinople! The young general began to dream even more. France was not quite ready for him; the expedition to Egypt on the other hand was offering him wide prospects, possibly exaggerated by Talleyrand. Everyone was relieved to see the impetuous "condottiere" go away: the Directors because they felt threatened by him, Talleyrand because it was too soon to consider seizing power, and the condottiere himself because his glory would thus remain intact. He would return when the time was ripe.

Accompanied by scholars and artists, the expedition secretly set sail for Egypt in May 1798. The English, who, for weeks, had been fearing to see the French fleet cruising in the Channel, could breath again once told it was sailing in the Mediterranean sea. Nelson, who was also there with a full squadron, chased it actively without success. It was fortunate for Napoleon, because on those ships which miraculously slipped through the English net, was an intellectual and military elite which would later contribute to the grandeur of the Empire... After sailing back to Egypt, Nelson destroyed Bonaparte's ships once his army had landed, stranding him in Egypt with his troops and cutting off all lines of communication with France.

The Egypt of the Mamelukes, theoretically a fief of the Sublime Porte, was independent and medieval in practice. The most splendid horsemen in the world, dressed in their sumptuous costumes, charged bravely and were massacred by the French cannons and muskets. Alexandria was taken without great resistance; then the expedition marched towards Cairo, enduring hideous suffering in the desert under a blistering July sun. At Giza, the Mamelukes were annihilated in a single battle, known as the battle of the Pyramids. Napoleon, whom the native population

called "Abounaparte," had become the master of Egypt. He acted there like an oriental despot, maintaining order with fierce repression.

"*Every day I have five or six heads lopped off in the streets of Cairo. We must adopt the tone necessary to make people obey...*"

Anxious to win the local religious authorities' favour, he showed tolerance for the Muslim religion. He knew that was indispensable to being accepted.

Egypt, however, was a restive mount that French "spurs" did not manage to tame. Popular revolts erupted, bloodily put down as in Italy, and the country did not take long, once Napoleon had departed, to free itself from its invaders.

Upset by the loss of their Egyptian province, the Turks, backed by the English, tried to go on the offensive. The French army attempted to catch them unawares by attacking Palestine then Syria. But Napoleon's oriental dream came to an end at Acre,

Next pages
The Battle of Aboukir, 7 Thermidor Year VII (July 25, 1799)

After the failure of Bonaparte's oriental dream at Acre, the retreat from Syria began. It became total war. Having lost the initiative, the conquerors had to hold out with the strength born of despair, and their suffering was marked out with brilliant victories such as Aboukir, close to where Nelson had destroyed their fleet.
Louis-Francois Lejeune (1775-1848), 1804.
Musée du Château de Versailles.

Pages 50-51
Bonaparte's Order of the day, 14 Thermidor Year VII (August 1, 1799), on the second Battle of Aboukir

Bonaparte describes the second Battle of Aboukir in this dispatch from Cairo which was printed in an edition of 75 under the control of Berthier, who ordered the plates destroyed afterwards. Bonaparte gave the greatest importance to the flow of information, and above all, to its contents, which he always carefully supervised or provided.
Printed in Cairo
Marc-Aurel.

which withstood eight assaults and broke his offensive. He had worded that dream in these amazing terms:

"If I succeed, as I believe, I shall find the pasha's treasures and weapons for three hundred thousand men. I shall stir up and arm the whole of Syria, and march on Damascus and Alep. As we advance in the country, I shall enlarge my army, with all of its malcontents. I shall announce to the people the abolition of servitude and of the tyrannical governments of the pashas. I shall reach Constantinople with armed masses. I shall overthrow the Turkish empire. I shall create a great new empire in the Orient that will truly establish my place in posterity, and I may return to Paris by way of Andrinople or Vienna, after having destroyed the House of Austria."

Foreshadowing the one from Russia, the retreat from Syria began. The wounded who could not be moved were abandoned in Jaffa and are said to have been finished off to prevent them from being caught alive by the enemy. According to certain sources, many Turkish prisoners had already been executed in cold blood. Two Ottoman armies were barely crushed at Mount Tabor and Aboukir. The conqueror had lost the initiative, and sought only to defend from outside attacks a country he no longer controlled.

France, after Corsica and Italy, seemed in fact the ideal country where he could fulfil his ambitions.

The news received from Paris convinced Napoleon that the Directory was in the throes of death. It had suffered severe military setbacks in Germany; the time had come: he had to seize the opportunity.

Preceded by the announcement of the victory at Aboukir, General Bonaparte abandoned his men to hurry back to France, slipping easily through the British squadrons. On October 9, 1799, he landed in Saint Raphaël bay.

The coup d'Etat of 18 Brumaire took place one month later.

The Battle of the Pyramids, 3 Thermidor Year VI (July 21, 1798)

A fief of the Sublime Porte, Mameluke's Egypt was independent in practice. These fierce warriors put up a bitter resistance. But Alexandria was more easily taken and the Mamelukes annihilated in one single battle at the Pyramids. Napoleon behaved afterwards like an oriental despot.
Louis-Francois Lejeune (1775-1848), dated 1806. Musée du château de Versailles.

Victoire d'Aboukir en Egypte, du 7. ther. an 7.

RÉPUBLIQUE

FRANÇAISE.

Au quartier-général du Kaire, le 25 thermidor an 7 de la République Française, une et indivisible.

ORDRE DU JOUR, du 25 thermidor an 7.

LE général *Songis* commande l'artillerie de l'armée.

Le citoyen *Samson*, chef de brigade du génie, est promu au grade de général de brigade, commandant l'arme du génie de l'armée.

L'adjudant-général *Sornet* est employé à l'état-major général de l'armée.

Cartel d'échange arrêté entre le Général MARMONT, *autorisé spécialement par le Général en Chef* BONAPARTE, *et le* PATRONA-BEY, *Commandant l'Escadre Turke.*

ART. I.er Les prisonniers respectifs seront échangés homme pour homme et grade pour grade.

II. Les blessés et chirurgiens ne seront point censés être prisonniers de guerre.

III. Tous les prisonniers Français actuellement existans à Constantinople et dans les différentes places de l'empire de Turkie, seront transportés d'ici à trois mois, et plutôt si cela se peut, sur des bâtimens, devant le port d'Alexandrie : à la même époque un même nombre de prisonniers Turks seront transférés à Alexandrie, et on procédera à l'échange d'après les articles I et II.

IV. Toutes les fois que des bâtimens turks, ayant à bord des prisonniers français, viendront devant Alexandrie, et feront connaître au commandant de cette place le nombre de prisonniers qu'ils ont à échanger, le commandant français sera tenu de représenter un même nombre de prisonniers turks, dans l'espace de soixante-douze heures, afin que l'on puisse sur-le-champ procéder à l'échange.

A Alexandrie, le 18 thermidor an 7 de la République.

Le GÉNÉRAL EN CHEF est mécontent du général *Zayonschek* qui a mis de la négligence dans l'exécution de l'ordre réitéré de faire partir pour le quartier-général le 3.e bataillon de la 22.me demi-brigade d'infanterie légère ; le général *Zayonschek*, commandant une province directement sous ses ordres, n'a aucune excuse à alléguer. Le GÉNÉRAL EN CHEF ordonne au général *Zayonschek*, de garder les arrêts pendant vingt-quatre heures. Immédiatement après la réception du présent ordre, il lui est ordonné de faire embarquer et partir pour le Kaire le 3.º bataillon de la 22.me demi-brigade d'infanterie légère.

Signé ALEXANDRE BERTHIER, *Général de Division Chef de l'Etat-major général.*

Au quartier-général d'Alexandrie, le 14 thermidor an 7 de la République Française, une et indivisible.

ORDRE DU JOUR du 14 thermidor an 7.

BONAPARTE, GÉNÉRAL EN CHEF,

Le nom d'Abou-Qyr était funeste à tout Français ; la journée du 7 thermidor l'a rendu glorieux : la victoire que l'armée vient de remporter accélère son retour en Europe.

Nous avons conquis Mayence et la limite du Rhin, en envahissant une partie de l'Allemagne, nous venons de reconquérir aujourd'hui nos établissemens aux Indes, et ceux de nos alliés. Par une seule opération, nous avons remis dans les mains du Gouvernement le pouvoir d'obliger l'Angleterre, malgré ses triomphes maritimes, à une paix glorieuse pour la République.

Nous avons beaucoup souffert : nous avons eu à combattre des ennemis de toute espèce ; nous en aurons encore à vaincre : mais enfin le résultat sera digne de nous, et nous méritera la reconnaissance de la patrie.

BONAPARTE.

Signé ALEXANDRE BERTHIER, *Général de Division, Chef de l'Etat-major général.*

Pour copie conforme au registre d'ordre ;

Towards the Coronation: 1799-1804

Brumaire Year VIII
(November 9 and 10, 1799)

Any other general but Napoleon would have been questioned about this unexpected return to France. But he was arriving in Paris at the very moment when the Directory was expiring under the attacks of various opposition parties, from the royalists, rather powerful in the West and South of France, to the Jacobins, dreaming of a Republic that would belong to them. The rats were already leaving the sinking ship. Sieyès, one of the five Directors, had prepared a coup d'Etat thinking he had the backing of General Joubert, who was untimely killed during the summer of 1799. Barras was feeling insecure and toying with the idea of a possible restoration of the monarchy. Everyone was waiting for an opportunity to act.

Appearing before the Directory to justify his unexpected return, Napoleon declared suavely:

"What struck me most was that your misfortunes were put down to my absence..."

He would also swear, pointing at the Turkish scimitar hanging at his side and which he used as a sword:

"Citizen Directors, I swear that I shall draw this sword only for the defense of the Republic and of its government."

Those listening, each in his own way, needed him too much to want him eliminated. Glorified by his victory at Aboukir, the young conqueror of Italy seemed to be the man they needed, the one who could become the arbiter of the internal struggles all parties were involved in. Although a military defeat, the expedition to Egypt had borne political fruit in the end. Bonaparte had not been sullied by the Directory's dishonest compromises and was considered by the people to be then the only undefeated general. The scent of adventure and fame which clung to him, as well as his youth, made him the man they needed.

Moreover, to guide him, there was always Monsieur de Talleyrand.

"Persuaded to resign" in July 1799, the Minister of Foreign Affairs never left Paris, and carefully

The morning of 18 Brumaire Year VIII (November 9, 1799)

*The plan for the coup was to give legally to Bonaparte the responsibility for the safety of the nation's representatives and to put all the troops from the Paris military division under his command. Anticipating this decision, the general had invited a number of high-ranking officers to call at his home at the break of day. He is shown here on the steps of the mansion in rue de la Victoire. Bonaparte is holding the decree from the Council of Elders in his hand and asking the assembled officers to save the Republic. They acclaim him as their provisional leader; at ten o'clock Bonaparte will take the loyalty oath before the Council of Elders but the most difficult part will be played the next day at Saint-Cloud where Lucien Bonaparte will save in extremis his brother, from a fatal failure.
Champion del.,
Lith. by Ch. Motte.*

monitored the accelerating decay of the Directory. Unpopularity, corruption, military setbacks, and a disastrous management of public affairs were sealing

the fate of the five "kings" of the Directory before long. Which side to choose then? Which side to favour? Which side would offer the best guarantees?

Roederer, Regnault, Boulay de la Meurthe, Maret and Fouché (already the Police minister) came and called on Napoleon to update him on the political situation and to sound him out. Two years before, it was the Orient *"that was waiting for one man;"* today it was France.

Bonaparte despised Barras for his cynicism and his compromised principles, and considered him finished as a politician. The Jacobins might have attracted him more, but Bernadotte, Désirée Clary's husband, was hostile to him. Sieyès, who wanted to reform the Constitution by the sword, was temporarily saved by his old project, as Talleyrand had him in mind to help Bonaparte "reintegrate" politics.

The main problem was that, although the two men needed each other, they were definitely loath to admit it. They took every opportunity to display their mutual disdain and contempt; it took the "devotion" and skill of Talleyrand, who was playing double or quits, to bring them to conspire together. The crucial meeting took place at the beginning of November. Everything was happening at once from then on.

Sensing a shift in the wind, Barras came and pledged allegiance, and then offered his services. Bonaparte was to be one of the three future Consuls, with Sieyès and Ducos; Sieyès still believed in a parliamentary coup in which the military will play but a minor part. Back into favour in spite of a tenderly kept lover, Joséphine was immersing herself into an intense social life and organizing sumptuous parties, while Talleyrand was making the rounds of the Parisian drawing-rooms looking for new accomplices. Fouché was swearing to the Directors that he had heard of nothing and that he would be the first one to know if something was really going to happen. Which was absolutely true, since he was part of the conspiracy.

The coup itself would last two days, the 18 and 19 Brumaire Year VIII (November 9 and 10, 1799). Alerted by one of their members, the Council of Elders decreed that it would move to Saint-Cloud to be *"sheltered from surprises and raids."* This would have been a wise precaution had General Bonaparte not been in charge of *"the execution of the present decree."* Napoleon made his way to the Tuileries where the Elders were still in session, to reassure them that he would stop *"those who would want trouble and disorder."* Generals Berthier, Marmont, Lefebvre etc. vouched for these good intentions. Bernadotte had stayed at home.

Napoleon delivered a fiery speech to the soldiers, whose real feelings were unknown to the conspirators:

"To listen to a few seditious voices, we would soon appear as enemies of the Republic, we who have strengthened it by our work and our courage!"

These words achieved the desired effect, and the troops marched with the conspirators. At the same time, Sieyès and Ducos stepped down from their positions as Directors while Barras, terrorized and "convinced" by Talleyrand, vacated his position, eagerly declaring that *"he was joyfully returning to the rank of plain citizen."* Moved by such good will, the former bishop "forgot" to hand over to the Director the three millions he had been given to overcome his last scruples...

A corrupt and mediocre head of state, Barras had brought about his own downfall by protecting the career of those who were deposing him then, as he was no longer useful.

The second act took place the following day at the château of Saint-Cloud "protected" by 6,000 armed men led by Murat. Indecision wafted in the air. Tired of waiting for the Elders to ratify the resignation of the Directory, Napoleon walked into the meeting hall. His appearance caused a sensation and upset those who were not in the know. The general knew better how to harangue his soldiers than politicians: his speech was so muddled and confused that he was jeered off.

"Follow me, I am the god of the day!" he would declare, among other things.

Deeply distraught in fact, Napoleon, accompanied by his old guard, went to the Council of Five Hundred gathered in the orangerie of the château, determined to stake his all.

Lucien Bonaparte, the president of the Assembly, tried in vain to calm the infuriated deputies. He had the presence of mind to step down from his official function, a move which suspended the session and prevented a vote outlawing Napoleon. *"No dictatorship!"* the frantic deputies were crying, *"we are free here! Bayonets do not frighten us!"*

Seeing his general suddenly stagger out, Murat immediately ordered his grenadiers: *"Get the whole lot out of there!"* while Lucien, brandishing a sword in a theatrical gesture, swore that he would run his brother through with it *"if he aspired to tyranny."*

Broken up by the "bayonets," the deputies spilt out into the garden tripping over their togas, which were ill-adapted for running. Sieyés's plan was ruined by the intervention of the army. The very evening, Bonaparte, who had pulled himself together, had become the leader of the conspiracy and one of the three new Consuls. Ducos designated him to head the government; Sieyés did not dare oppose the move. Paris, which had lost its revolutionary fervour, meekly accepted the change of régime.

"The farce is over," wrote a sarcastic Réal, while Talleyrand, nonchalant and getting back to the basics, was recommending to his friends:

"We should have dinner now…"

Lebrun. The real power was in the sole hands of the First Consul, with the full support of Talleyrand:

"You must be First Consul, and the First Consul must control all that is directly related to government policy, that is the ministry of the Interior and of Police for domestic affairs and my ministry (Foreign Relations) for foreign affairs, then the two grand means of action: War and the Navy."

Justice and Finance will be entrusted to subordinates; *"that will amuse them and keep them busy while you, General, having all the vital parts of the government at your disposition, you will achieve the noble goal you have set: the regeneration of France."*

The reorganization of the country: 1800-1802

"… Napoleon emerged from Bonaparte."

This is more than a witty remark: it expresses a reality, as the adventurer of the Revolution was succeeded by an exceptional head of state.

The transition was not immediate nevertheless: Napoleon had already ruled in Italy, then in Egypt, but France could not be governed like a conquered country. Its miserable condition was calling for an in-depth reorganization of its structures, which would integrate the lessons of the Revolution while preparing for the future. Quickly edged out, Sieyès and Ducos were replaced by two docile Consuls: Cambacérès and

This "regeneration" began with the promulgation of a new Constitution, purposely "short and obscure," widely inspired mainly by Sieyès, Lebrun and Gaudin, and drafted so as to not hinder the First Consul, who was impetuously declaring:

"It is I who govern and I shall hold power to my last breath."

But he was also adding:

"My policy is to govern men as the majority of them want it. […] If I were governing a Jewish nation, I would rebuild the temple of Solomon."

Napoleon intended to rule alone and quickly set up the foundations of his dictatorship, controlling the press and replacing the two Councils of the Directory with four new bodies (the Senate, the Legislative

**One franc of Year XI
(1802-1803):
Bonaparte
First Consul /
French Republic**

*In February 1800, Bonaparte
created the Bank of France,
which had the monopoly of
printing paper money, now
accepted by the people as
confidence has been restored.
The mint, on the other hand,
was striking coins of which this
franc from Year XI is a
magnificent example.*
Musée de la Monnaie.

One franc of Year XI (1802-1803): Bonaparte First Consul / French Republic

This remarkable work was done by the chief engraver Pierre-Joseph Tiolier, who started his tenure that very year and will remain then until September 1816. The coin was minted in the Paris workshops managed by Charles-Pierre de l'Espine, whose symbol was a rooster.
Musée de la Monnaie

Body, the Tribunate and the Council of State) which had no freedom to act. The Council of State was to assume the responsibility of preparing the laws, the Tribunate to discuss them without the power to either accept or reject them, and the Legislature to vote for them without discussion. The role of the Senate was to appoint the members of the other three bodies and to make sure the Constitution was upheld.

The recruitment of the members of the new government was fast and without argument. Lebrun, the Second Consul, owed his nomination to the well-written dedications of his translations of Tasso and Homer. Gaudin, Minister of Finance, was similarly recruited after rather restrained proceedings:

— *"Have you worked for a long time in Finance?*

— *For twenty years, General.*

— *We need your help badly, and I count on it. Go on, take the oath. We are in a hurry."*

The new Constitution went into effect on December 25, 1799, a month and a half after the coup d'Etat. Events were going fast, too fast in the eyes of the former revolutionaries who were bitterly stressing that the people had not even been consulted! But it was no longer the point, as Cabanis stressed:

"The ignorant classes will no longer wield any influence either on the legislation or on the government; everything is done for the people and in the name of the people, nothing is done by the people under their unconsidered dictates."

Nobody stood up and challenged the new developments. Weary of the chaos that followed the Revolution, the French had no cause yet for complaint about their new master's strong arm, a strong man they were unconsciously calling for after all these years of anarchy.

On that same December 25, the First Consul announced his program to the Council of State:

"The romance of the Revolution is now over, we must start to write its history and look only at what can be possibly achieved when implementing its principles [...] We must make the Republic dear to its citizens, respectable to foreigners, and frightening to its enemies."

The program was all the more ambitious as the country was on the verge of complete ruin. The administration and finances were totally disorganized; election to all public offices has led to the tyranny of a violent minority over a timid majority; only forced loans with derisory returns were funding the budget of the State... There was runaway inflation, paper money (the Assignats) no longer inspired confidence, and insecurity was reigning supreme both in cities, deprived of police force, and in the countryside, where highwaymen could operate with complete impunity.

The first thing to do was to provide the State with means of action, starting with the reorganization of the country's finances, hence of the collection of taxes. Financial circles had contributed to the coup d'Etat of Brumaire; they were no doubt disappointed to learn that only 167,000 miserable francs were left in the Treasury. At the end of 1799, the old elected officials were replaced with men appointed by the State.

Bonaparte put at the top of the hierarchy the Minister of Finance responsible for the assessment and collection of taxes, and the Minister of the Treasury, responsible for the allocation of funds and public expenditure. These two men ruled over controllers, collectors and inspectors, and the conflicts of interest which regularly opposed them helped ensure a sound management of public finances.

Napoleon also thought about creating a financial establishment that would belong to the State and would take on the task of issuing money backed by a considerable capital to ensure its credibility. This institution would allow the State both to establish its control over money and to free itself from the supervision of the most powerful financiers. The Bank of France was founded in May 1800, as a result of these thoughts.

The reforms were carried out briskly according to the same procedure: elimination of all those "elected" by the Directory, who had proven their incompetence, and reorganization of the very structures of the State taking into account the lessons taught by the Revolution. Prefects were to head departments, sub-prefects arrondissements, and mayors municipalities. In March 1800, the judiciary too was altered in order to reinforce the authority of the central government. The hand of the First Consul could be felt everywhere, improving what could be kept of the apparatus of the government and doing away with the rest.

Domestic peace was another area requiring particular attention from the new régime. As long as social unrest and political parties, not to mention the royal uprising in Vendée in the west, were not put down, the Consulate would not be able to carry out the reforms imagined by Bonaparte. He was moving toward a solitary exercise of power, having reduced the assemblies to their simplest expression. The dramatic circumstances in which he had seized power persuaded the different sides to be patient. They viewed the First Consul as a transitional figure who could put the country on its feet again, while uniting the past to the present. The very attitude of Napoleon, who was seeking political support from all parties, was reinforcing their analysis.

"To govern in a party, he was saying, is to fall, sooner or later, under its influence. I shall not fall for it. I am national."

This frame of mind was no doubt the best the ruler of a country ruined and devastated by internecine quarrels, as was France in 1800, could be in. An expedition was sent to the west, under the orders of General Brune, to bring the Royalists back on the right track. But the truce which was reached was not genuine. The religious issue was still the Achilles' heel of the Consulate, even though churches were reopened and émigrés were gradually returning, as old loyalties, either revolutionary or monarchist, were still alive. People were putting up with the Consulate more than they were adhering to it.

Peace abroad was also desirable for a government which was directing its efforts towards national reconstruction. The country needed to get its breath back and had temporarily put aside the spirit of conquest so cherished by the Revolution. As early as December 1799, Napoleon had written to the sovereigns of the Coalition powers. A disdainful silence had been their only answer.

Even worse, war had started again while Napoleon was busy subduing the last Chouans in the west and sorting out the administrative chaos.

Backed by England, Austria had launched attacks simultaneously in Italy and Germany.

Moreau had been sent to Germany, but had been quickly forced to cross back the Rhine, while Masséna was in a difficult situation and got trapped in Genoa. Napoleon decided to go on the offensive in Lombardy so as to strike at the heart of the enemy deployments.

In May 1800, the First Consul left to join the army he had ordered assembled in Dijon to rescue Italy. The crossing of the Grand-Saint-Bernard pass ensued and the fate of the new régime was decided at the battle of Marengo, on June 14, 1800. Fought against Austrians who were superior in numbers, that battle was won at the last minute thanks to the arrival of Desaix, who launched a desperate attack against Austrians who already thought they were victorious. Desaix, lost his life there, but saved the Consulate.

After having prepared a successor to Napoleon who was unwisely away from the Tuileries, Paris jubilantly welcomed his return. The thirty-one-year-old dictator was finally accepted by the French people.

Austria believed it could continue the war, but its troops were crushed a second time by Moreau in the Hohenlinden forest (on December 3, 1800), forcing it to negotiate. On February 9, 1801, the Treaty of Lunéville put an end to hostilities. France secured possession of its "natural limits," the Rhine, the Alps and the Pyrenees; it also forced Austria to recognize the Batavian, Helvetic, Cisalpine and Ligurian Republics as French protectorates. Vienna also had to accept the reorganization by France of the German empire.

Overtures made to Russia had been welcomed by Czar Paul I, who had reconsidered his hostility of 1799. But this promising alliance, which would be renewed at Tilsit, depended in fact on the Czar's life, just as the Consulate depended on Napoleon's one. Worried to see Paul turn against them, the English plotted his assassination with a few members of the russian elite, who were infuriated by the Czar's madness and an ukase closing Russian ports to British ships. In March 1801, Paul I was strangled and succeeded by his son Alexander to the great relief of everyone, but the First Consul. The new Czar was twenty-three and wanted to bring happiness to his subjects. He therefore did not worry too much about sending troops abroad. That time would come…

Napoleon concluded valuable alliances with Spain, Naples, the United States, Algiers and Tunis…

Next pages
The Crossing of the Grand-Saint-Bernard Pass by the French army on May 20, 1800

In May 1800, the First Consul left to join the army sent to rescue Italy. The crossing of this pass, a highlight of Napoleonic mythology, led to the difficult victory over the Austrians at Marengo.
Charles Thévenin (1764-1838), 1808.
Musée du château de Versailles.

against England, which persisted in waging war. Great-Britain, which had won in that war everything it could have possibly wanted, but was facing a deteriorating political situation on the home front, finally decided to seek peace. The resignation of William Pitt had a lot to do with it, and his return to power in 1803 would call everything into question.

The Peace of Amiens was signed on March 27, 1802, to the great relief of both countries. It would be however only a break in a war that would last more than twenty years (1793-1815).

Another conflict would last as long as the Empire: the one which would oppose it to the Holy See.

The First Consul knew that domestic peace would never really be established as long as religion would remain a stumbling block between the various political sides. The church had been hard hit by the Revolution. Its property had been sold, its priests "converted" to the Revolution or hunted down, its States invaded by the French armies. But faith was still alive in France, and remained the social cement necessary for the reconstruction of the society envisioned by Napoleon.

"A society without religion is like a ship without a compass; it is religion alone that gives the State a firm and durable support."

The attempt of the French Revolution to establish a Church of France subservient to the State had not brought very good results. It was quite the opposite indeed, as the issue of that degraded and humiliated Church was indeed the oldest quarrels between political parties.

"To put an end to that disorder, we had to put back religion on its base, which could only be done by measures acknowledged by the very religion. Lessons learnt from history and reason commanded to resort to the Supreme Pontiff to bring opposite opinions together and reconcile hearts."

The old revolutionaries were not following the same line of thought, and negotiations with the Holy See started in a tense domestic situation.

Pius VII did nothing to make them easier. He was quite willing to "forgive" France's past sins, but his forgiveness was depending on a certain number of conditions.

Bonaparte signing the Concordat on July 16, 1801

Anxious to close up the still fresh scars left by the dechristianisation policy of the Revolution and to stop the quarrels over the issue of the Church of France subservient to the State, Bonaparte forced the Pope's hand by using the threat of a possible invasion of the Pontifical States. The message was well received and the Concordat signed by the papal representative, Cardinal Consalvi, four days after the friendly intervention of the First Consul.
Baron François Gérard (1770-1837).
Musée du château de Versailles.

Negotiations were long and painful. Napoleon had to bay and to issue an ultimatum to the Pope's representative, Cardinal Consalvi, on June 12. Rome had every reason to take this ultimatum seriously: France was ruling Italy and could easily invade the Pontifical States. The message was well received, and the Concordat was signed on July 16.

That document specified that the Roman Catholic religion was the religion of the great majority of the French people, that there will be freedom of worship, that bishops would be appointed by the government, that Rome would institute them and that they would become public servants paid by the State to which they would pledge allegiance.

Another major concession given by Rome was that the sale of the Church property that had taken place since 1789 was irrevocable and that the buyers would not have to return them. That was one thing the Consulate could not dare to go back on. Louis XVIII would not show such wisdom during the First Restoration.

The Concordat was accepted in France because all moderate minds viewed it as an instrument of peace, a willingness to come to terms with the majority. Only a few die-hard Republicans continued to criticize this act of political wisdom. On leaving Notre-Dame, a general told to the First Consul:

"It was a fine monkish show. It only lacked the presence of the million men who gave their lives to put an end to what you are now reinstating!"

Napoleon let people talk. This agreement with Rome legitimized his regime and represented an important step towards domestic peace and stability he was striving to reestablish. Pius VII was in fact cursing the First Consul while pretending to be his ally.

Neither of them had said their final word on the subject. Within two years, and thanks to exceptional advisers, Napoleon had managed to restore the French domestic and foreign affairs to order. The economy, bankrupt in 1799, was slowly starting up again. The new institutions had given the regime a solid base that allowed it to pursue long-term policies; finally, the constant danger of foreign aggression had been temporarily pushed aside, which was an invaluable success. In the spring of 1802, republican France was governed by a dictatorship which was preparing the country for the Empire. Appointed Consul for life on August 2, 1802, its master too was getting ready for it.

Consul for life: 1802-1804

On December 24, 1800 the First Consul had been the victim of an assassination attempt in rue Saint-Nicaise while on its way to the Opera. He barely escaped. A few suspects were then deported. Napoleon was convinced that the authors of the attempt were anarchist "terrorists," but Fouché was inclined to favour a Royalist plot, which later turned out to be true. Those guilty were captured and executed, and the anarchists remained in deportation because they were *"basically bad men."*

The attack had physically missed its target, but had left nevertheless considerable repercussions. It had underlined the succession issue which had already been raised when the First Consul went to fight against the Austrians in Italy. Fouché and Talleyrand had been plotting then "just in case" he did not return. They had

naturally given away their accomplices (including Senator Clément de Ris) to their master upon his return, to prove that their loyalty to him remained intact. Their pretence of allegiance obviously did not fool Napoleon, but he needed these two men too much to afford to get rid of them. Such plots will reappear every time the Emperor would tempt his fate in a great battle, far from Paris and from his entourage. One day the conspirators will have it their way…

The problem of succession remained unresolved after the assassination attempt of rue Saint-Nicaise, and it dawned on everyone that the recovery of the country was depending, if not on a man, at least on the continuity of the system of government he had striven to set up. The hereditary nature of power, the establishment of a dynasty which could revive the monarchist pomp were in everybody's mind. The Interior Minister and a brilliant politician, Lucien Bonaparte was willingly spreading these ideas which were serving his own ambitions. His enthusiasm, his lack of prudence and his eagerness to possibly succeed the First Consul, led the latter to send his brother to Spain and to keep him at a distance forever.

Napoleon himself was considering that possibility, but hardly spoke of it, reluctant to take the plunge. Although Talleyrand willingly encouraged him in this way, the First Consul was waiting for public opinion, still marked by ten years of Revolution, to become somewhat more mature. Opposition to these projects was rather strong as the supporters of the consular oligarchy were reluctant to see the establishment of an "individual" dictatorship. The Legislative Body and the Tribunate were grumbling so loudly that Napoleon grew angry with their resistance. Some bills, in particular the details of the Civil Code, were too heatedly discussed for the easily offended First Consul:

"My clothes are infested with vermin; but do they really believe that I shall let them push me around as they did with Louis XVI?" he would exclaim.

That opposition of intellectuals and generals, which had no popular support, was in fact easily silenced. Even Fouché, suspected of not subscribing to the project of Life Consulate, was forced out of the police. He would come back later after having spent some time *"driveling in the Senate,"* in the words of the future Emperor.

BULLETIN DES LOIS.

N.º I.

(N.º 1.) *SÉNATUS-CONSULTE ORGANIQUE,*

Du 28 Floréal an XII.

NAPOLÉON, par la grâce de Dieu et les constitutions de la République, EMPEREUR DES FRANÇAIS, à tous présens et à venir, SALUT.

Le Sénat, après avoir entendu les orateurs du Conseil d'État, a décrété et nous ORDONNONS ce qui suit :

EXTRAIT des registres du Sénat conservateur, du 28 Floréal an XII de la République.

LE SÉNAT CONSERVATEUR, réuni au nombre de membres prescrit par l'article 90 de la Constitution ; vu le projet de sénatus-consulte rédigé en la forme prescrite par l'article 57 du sénatus-consulte organique en date du 16 thermidor an X ;

Après avoir entendu, sur les motifs dudit projet, les orateurs du Gouvernement, et le rapport de sa commission spéciale, nommée dans la séance du 26 de ce mois;

L'adoption ayant été délibérée au nombre de voix prescrit par l'article 56 du sénatus-consulte organique du 16 thermidor an X,

1. *IV.ᵉ Série.*   A

(2)

DÉCRÈTE ce qui suit :

TITRE PREMIER.

ART. I.ᵉʳ LE GOUVERNEMENT DE LA RÉPUBLIQUE est confié à un Empereur, qui prend le titre d'EMPEREUR DES FRANÇAIS.

La justice se rend, au nom de l'EMPEREUR, par les officiers qu'il institue.

2. NAPOLÉON BONAPARTE, Premier Consul actuel de la République, est EMPEREUR DES FRANÇAIS.

TITRE II.

De l'Hérédité.

3. La dignité impériale est héréditaire dans la descendance directe, naturelle et légitime de NAPOLÉON BONAPARTE, de mâle en mâle, par ordre de primogéniture, et à l'exclusion perpétuelle des femmes et de leur descendance.

4. NAPOLÉON BONAPARTE peut adopter les enfans ou petits-enfans de ses frères, pourvu qu'ils aient atteint l'âge de dix-huit ans accomplis, et que lui-même n'ait point d'enfans mâles au moment de l'adoption.

Ses fils adoptifs entrent dans la ligne de sa descendance directe.

Si, postérieurement à l'adoption, il lui survient des enfans mâles, ses fils adoptifs ne peuvent être appelés qu'après les descendans naturels et légitimes.

L'adoption est interdite aux successeurs de NAPOLÉON BONAPARTE et à leurs descendans.

5. A défaut d'héritier naturel et légitime ou d'héritier adoptif de NAPOLÉON BONAPARTE, la dignité impériale est dévolue et déférée à *Joseph Bonaparte* et à ses descendans naturels et légitimes, par ordre de primogéniture, et de mâle en mâle, à l'exclusion perpétuelle des femmes et de leur descendance.

After a long debate, the Civil Code was finally enacted on March 21, 1804. It was based upon personal freedom, the freedom to work, and the equality of all in the eyes of the law. It was thus respecting the principles of 1789, with however a few adjustments aimed a reinforcing the structures of the "new" society Napoleon wanted to build: women were treated like minors, divorce laws tightened and illegitimate children excluded from inheritance. This Code, which is still in force in its broad outlines, sanctioned the rise to power of the bourgeoisie and of its fundamental values: liberty, equality, property. It allowed the future Emperor to win the support of the middle classes and of the peasants by preventing a return to the laws of the Ancien Régime.

Everything was ready for the Empire: Napoleon had reformed the administration, stabilized the country's finances, imposed peace on his terms with Austria and England, and endowed the state with a solid body of laws flexible enough to be sometimes dispensed with. That was the responsibility of the Senate. The guardian of the Constitution, it had also the power to amend it if necessary; and its debates had the advantage of not being public. Hence the procedure of "sénatus - consulte," which helped in fact to do without laws, and allowed the country to move imperceptibly towards an absolute imperial power.

The official propaganda was thoroughly manipulating the masses: Napoleon created a real cult around himself and his policies, based upon undeniable results and a budding legend that was skillfully maintained. The Journal de Paris was thus stating in all seriousness:

"The prodigious strength of the First Consul's body allows him to work eighteen hours a day, allows him to focus his attention during these eighteen hours on a single subject, or on twenty in a row, and neither the difficulty of a given subject nor the physical drain involved prevent him from studying another one..."

The people, the army, the leading citizens were starting to feel attachment to their First Consul, forgetting Marengo and the plunder of Italy to remember only Brumaire and Arcole. At the same time, the former Royalists, in favour of the monarchical drift of the regime, were moving closer to those Brumairians most convinced of the need to bolster the executive power.

On May 6, 1802, the Tribunate called for a national plebiscite on the question: *"Should Napoleon Bonaparte be Consul for life?"* The results were exhilarating: 3,653,600 "yes" against 8,272 "no." The latter figures, coming mostly from the army, were under specific instructions:

"The first of you who does not vote for the Consulate for life, a general was paternally explaining to his men, I shall have him shot in front of the regiment."

This success set Napoleon on the way to coronation: he began to behave like a crowned sovereign, reintroduced customs and formalities that had not been used for ages, prohibited familiar forms of address, set up his court and its costumes... The Legion of Honor was created at that time, distinctly recalling, with the color of its red ribbon, the Royal Order of Saint-Louis...

The Royalists were defeat. They concocted a new conspiracy, led by General Pichegru which Cadoudal and Moreau, the victor at Hohenlinden, had rallied to. The affair could have had historical consequences, but a secret agent of the Police helped expose the plot. The leaders of the conspiracy were quickly arrested, and one of their men confessed they were waiting for a "prince" to carry out their plan.

It had been an ominous warning sign, and an exasperated Napoleon had flown into a murderous rage.

"Am I simply a dog one can batter to death in the street... while my murderers will be held sacrosanct! They attack my person! I shall return blow for blow!"

That mysterious "prince" was believed to be —or so was one willing to believe— the duc d'Enghien, the last in the line of the House of Condé. The young man was living near the border, in the territory of Baden, with a small court of émigrés. During the night of March 14 to 15, 1804, a small detachment of cavalry including Caulaincourt crossed the Rhine. The prisoner was taken under guard to Vincennes. But what should be done with him?

"The House of Bourbon must be taught that the blows it aims at others may backfire!" Napoleon declared, eager to get the message across to those who would attempt again to assassinate him. Interrogated during the night of March 20, Enghien, after a brief trial, was shot in the moat of the château de Vincennes.

Only the Jacobins would applaud the execution of the prince. At the last minute, Napoleon had been willing to postpone the execution, but the orders came too late. A mistake has been made.

That event created a definite uneasiness long-lasting. It would leave an indelible stain on the consciences of its organizers and protagonists. Napoleon would never be able to justify himself completely; Talleyrand would not manage to destroy the pieces of evidence that were overwhelmingly incriminating him. Caulincourt would be poorly received by the Czar years later, when sent on a mission to him…

Quickly put down, the conspiracy of Year XII led unintentionally to a propaganda campaign aimed at establishing a stronger power base for the First Consul. A docile Tribunate proposed to solve the problem of succession by conferring an imperial title on Napoleon and his family. A new Constitution was drawn up in record time, laying the foundations of the Empire.

It was welcomed by public opinion because it gave satisfactory answers to the question of succession and ensured the stability of power. Plots, assassination attempts, became irrelevant as the head of state's death would not call the very existence of the regime into question. New imperial dignitaries appeared (Grand Chamberlain, Grand Elector, etc.), as well as the first Marshals: Berthier, Murat, Masséna, Augereau,

Bernadotte… The embryo of the future imperial nobility, a cast of a privileged few close to the Emperor, was gradually building up.

Anxious to have his legitimacy based on popular approval, Napoleon ordered a new plebiscite: there were 3,572,329 "yes" against 2,569 "no." The new imperial family was naturally in favour of that elevation, but to different degrees. Lucien, the most brilliant, had been purely and simply dropped from the imperial succession; only the descendants of Napoleon, of Joseph and of Louis could inherit the imperial title. This arrangement did not satisfy the sisters of the future Emperor: their children would not be "princes." They complained so much that Napoleon would exclaim one day: *"It really seems, to listen to my sisters, that I have defrauded my family of the inheritance of the late king, our father!"*

The most delicate problem was not finally to convince the French, but to bring Pius VII to Notre-Dame. Only the Pope could give the coronation the symbolic value the First Consul wanted it to be endowed with. He would confer the future Emperor a spiritual legitimacy he could not disregard, because he would appear as nothing more than an adventurer without it. Pius VII hesitated and needed a great deal of convincing. Negotiations started again and finally ended in the anticipated result: the Pope would crown the Emperor. The ceremony took place in Paris on December 2, 1804. It was the revenge of Canossa.

Charles Maurice de Talleyrand-Périgord at the coronation of Emperor Napoleon, on December 2, 1804 (detail)

The prelate who instigated the nationalization of church property would always know how to look after, if not to influence —as on 18 Brumaire— Bonaparte's destiny. At the time of coronation, the Foreign Affairs minister had not yet betrayed his master. The Consul for life was then worried about another bishop, the one in Rome. The Pope's presence was indispensable to confer the future Emperor a spiritual legitimacy he could not disregard. The Pope was eventually convinced. He consecrated Napoleon, but because he would appear as nothing more than adventurer without it. Napoleon took the crown from the Pope's hands and crowned himself, showing thus the origin of his power. Louis David (1748-1825). Musée du Louvre.

THE EMPEROR
1804-1815

The visionary conqueror: 1804-1812

The height of power: 1804-1807

The period of conquests

The peace with England had lasted only a year. In the spring of 1803, the First Consul had strongly criticized Lord Whitworth, the English ambassador, for not respecting the Treaty of Amiens which made provision for British troops to evacuate Malta. The ambassador had haughtily replied that France had not evacuated Holland and that the annexation of Piedmont and the seizure of Switzerland by France in the meantime had not been provided for in the agreement. Napoleon flew into a rage, calling the occupation of Switzerland and Piedmont "a mere trifle," and threatened the Englishman with an attack on his country.

England was uneasily watching the rapid recovery of a France it had thought permanently ruined. All in all, the Cabinet in London concluded, war exhausts Great Britain but does nothing to strengthen France. The non observance of the commitments made in Amiens demonstrated furthermore the precarious nature of a treaty only favoured by specific circumstances. A confrontation had become inevitable.

As a landing in England needed time to prepare, Napoleon chose to begin by attacking Hanover, a continental possession of King George III, and the Achilles' heel of Great Britain. He took advantage of the opportunity to complete the reorganization of Germany, which began at Rastadt in 1797 and was carried on at Lunéville. That reorganisation, which was weakening the influence of Austria in Germany to the benefit of the main German states such as Bavaria or Prussia, displeased England which was watching with concern France extend its control over Germany. The countries conquered by the Consulate meant fewer markets for the English manufacturers, as Napoleon had refused to sign the trade agreement outlined by the Treaty of Amiens. From then on, London was the soul of the resistance to French hegemony, acting as the "banker" of the different coalitions which it was bankrolling lavishly with its famous "subsidies."

The project of a descent on the British Isles, under preparation since 1804 in the "camp de Boulogne" where the invasion force was assembled, forced the British Cabinet to form a new coalition including Austria, Naples, Sweden and Russia, to divert the French threat from its shores. Only Prussia was remaining non-committal, trading its neutrality for Hanover. The duc d'Enghien's assassination in March 1804 had turned the Emperor of the French into the personal enemy of all of Europe's sovereigns, who hated him at least as much as they feared him.

At the end of September 1805, the Emperor left Saint-Cloud to join the Grande Armée in Strasbourg. He had hoped to dominate the seas, or at least to neutralize the British fleet, by securing Spain's assistance. The disaster of Trafalgar on October 21, 1805, established England's maritime domination. That would prove to be a decisive factor in the final defeat in the long run, as Great Britain would be able to strike where and when it wanted on the continent.

68

At the same time, the destruction of the French fleet reduced to nothing all the viable plans of a landing in England. The strategy of strangulation, of a continental blockade, would become a logical consequence of Trafalgar. No one could have guessed then that England had virtually won the war: it would take nearly another ten years to realize it.

The campaign of 1805, which began with the encirclement of the Austrian General Mack at Ulm, was brilliant. Misled and demoralized, Mack surrendered and allowed thus the French to further advance. On November 14, Napoleon was entering Vienna. The intervention of the Russians, joined by the remaining Austrian forces, ended on December 2,

Vienna were very stringent and allowed Napoleon to reorganize once again Germany by creating the kingdoms of Bavaria and Wurtemberg and turning a loose conglomeration of minor German princes into vassals anxious to join the victor's side.

On December 26, 1805, the Treaty of Pressburg (Talleyrand was one of the signatories) sanctioned the decline of Austria, which had to relinquish Venice, Dalmatia, Tyrol and Swabia to satellite states of the French Empire, which was itself expanding in the south of Italy with the control of Naples.

The creation of the Confederation of the Rhine regrouping most of the states in West and South Germany under French "protection" led to the destruction of the Holy Roman Empire founded by Charlemagne in the year 800. On August 6, 1806, Francis II had to renounce his title of German Emperor to become "only" Emperor Francis I of Austria.

Some hope for peace followed this lightning campaign, but neither Great Britain nor Russia had yet accepted their humiliation. In the summer of 1806, Prussia, considered then the foremost military power in Europe, decided to go to war against France.

Its lukewarm commitment during the battles of 1805 had brought the downfall of Napoleon's adversaries; imbued with the legacy of Frederick the Great, it probably expected to bring to heel the French conqueror who was then threatening its influence in Germany, while avenging the humiliation of Valmy. Obsessed by their haste to fight, the Prussians neglected to wait for their Russian ally and hurled their troops, split into three columns, at the Grande Armée. But Napoleon intercepted them before they could link up. On October 14, 1806, at Jena and Auerstaedt, the army of Frederick William III was annihilated.

On the 27th of that same month, the Emperor of the French entered Berlin, while his unfortunate adversary took refuge with the Czar. Napoleon quickly reorganized the former Prussian sphere of influence to his advantage, dividing Prussia itself into four departments, imposing a war "contribution" of 160 million francs, and elevating the elector of Saxony to King. Twenty years after the death of Frederick II, his kingdom was destroyed and practically wiped off the map, only surviving east of the Elbe river.

1805, in the crushing victory at Austerlitz, where Napoleon demonstrated his true genius. Alexander of Russia learnt at his expense that he would never be the strategist he dreamt to be.

These successes against the continental powers further accentuated the "land-based" character of the imperial hegemony. The terms of peace dictated at

The Victory at Austerlitz, on December 2, 1805

The intervention of fresh Russian and Austrian forces did not prevent the brilliant victory at Austerlitz, the epitome of the superiority of war intuition over academic rules.

The behaviour of the French victor, in 1806, would be the source of a century and a half of antagonism between Paris and Berlin.

There were still Russia and England. While in Berlin, Napoleon decreed the beginning of the Continental System, a blockade aimed at strangling the British economy by depriving it of its markets. As London was more of a threat with its "subsidies" than with its armies, as its fleet made an invasion on its soil impossible, the only solution was to ruin it. As for Russia, it would be brought to heel the following year.

Fought on February 8, 1807, the Battle of Eylau remained undecided and was won only thanks to the charge of Murat's eighty cavalry squadrons. Augereau lost his way in the snowstorm and his corps was wiped out. The battle was a sheer slaughter as reported in the *64th Bulletin of the Grande Armée*:

"After the Battle of Eylau, the Emperor spent everyday several hours on the battlefield, that horrible scene…"

Napoleon himself would write to the Empress: *"That sight should inspire rulers with the love of peace and the hatred of war."*

Danzig fell in March after a brief siege. The road to Poland was opened. Even if the Russians had been jostled at Eylau, they were however far from being defeated. The Grande Armée was cut off from its base and the outcome of the war remained undecided. Vienna was plotting behind its conqueror's back, while Spain's behaviour was ambiguous. The conscript class of 1808 was called up to make up for the losses at Eylau; the Stock Exchange was already shivering, and there were fears of a new financial crisis similar to the one in 1805.

After Marengo and Austerlitz, Napoleon knew that he would once again be risking the destinies of his empire in the next battle. After the failure of an Austrian attempt to mediate between Russia and France, military operations resumed with the arrival of spring.

Alexander and Frederick William had further strengthened their ties in Bartenstein with the blessing of England, which had promised one million pounds worth of subsidies and 200,000 soldiers. The outcome of the campaign was decided on June 14, 1807, the

Napoleon enters Berlin, on October 27, 1806

Prussia hardly tolerated the French influence in Germany. In the summer of 1806, she decided to go to war against France, and hurled its troops, split into three columns, against the Grande Armée. Napoleon intercepted them and on October 14, 1806, the army of Frederick William III was completely destroyed at Jena and Auerstadt. On the 27th, the Emperor entered Berlin.
Charles Maynier (1768-1832), Salon of 1810.
Musée du château de Versailles.

anniversary of the victory at Marengo. Driven back to the river Alle, the Russians were in too poor a position to effectively resist the massive attack directed against them.

The Battle of Friedland had been won.

François Vigo-Roussillon recounts:

"On the morning of June 17, the Emperor took the lead of the cavalry and crossed the river to the applause of the infantry which was watching. It was a magnificent thing to see: the sun was beating down on a line of twelve regiments of cuirassiers and two regiments of carabiniers; their weapons were dazzling the eye [...]. On the 19th, around five o'clock in the evening, we arrived at the city of Tilsit on the Niemen."

"The Russian army had set up camp on the other side of the river after burning its bridge. As the river could not be crossed, camps were set up around Tilsit. As soon as Napoleon arrived, the Emperor of Russia asked for a meeting. It took place in the middle of the river, an armistice was declared. It was agreed that, should any of the two armies decide to attack the other one, it would give it a one-month advance warning." At the time of his meeting with Alexander on the famous raft set up in the middle of the Niemen

the outcome of which appeared then a foregone conclusion. Alexander was thirty. He was idealistic and mercurial, getting carried away by causes he would abandon when they did not fire his imagination any more... or they threatened to materialize. The Czar, who had a complex personality, all at once mystical, chivalrous, generous and hot-tempered, would turn out to be Napoleon's greatest ally and his worst enemy.

They had been at war since 1805 when Alexander had thought he could become involved in European affairs. The initial hostility was followed by some respect which, during the days at Tilsit, would turn to a true, although partly calculated, friendship.

Napoleon needed urgently to finally make peace, Alexander to sign an acceptable peace treaty that would maintain part of Prussia. Each one wanted to charm the other: they managed to do so at England's expense. An apparently solid alliance was the immediate result of the peace proposals. Alexander agreed without reservation to the Continental System and accepted the creation of the Duchy of Warsaw; a touched Napoleon was unveiling to him, in a confidential tone, the great things they could achieve together. Bonaparte and Romanov were daydreaming together...

At St Helena, the fallen Emperor would remember that complicity:

"We would leave immediately after dinner under the pretext of some business to attend to at our camps; but Alexander and I would meet again soon after to have tea at his camp or at mine, and would stay together talking until midnight, and beyond..."

Fascinated by each other, the two young emperors were remapping the world, both literally and figuratively. Their relationship will later become ambiguous, sullied by political necessities and a mutual misunderstanding. Tilsit was their honeymoon.

"I never liked anyone more than him," Alexander would later say, while Napoleon, yet sparing of this kind of confession, would confide:

"I was content with him and I liked him..."

It was without doubt a genuine friendship, even though other factors contributed to encourage it. A year later, at Erfurt, Alexander would already be lying, unlike Napoleon who would still have the same feelings for him.

river, Napoleon was 38 years old and could claim, temporarily at least, to have subdued Europe. Italy, Germany, Austria, Prussia and Russia had all been subjugated or defeated, and Great Britain only, protected by its insularity, could persist in a struggle,

The fall of Magdeburg, on November 8, 1806

The crushing victory of the French over Frederick William III at Jena and Auerstaedt on October 14, demoralized the Prussian resistance. Magdeburg fell. The triumphant army, under Marshal Ney's command, entered the city. The French took 16,000 prisoners and 800 guns.
Colored engraving.
Paris, chez Jean,
10, rue Jean de Beauvais.

The Empire in 1807

Those few days in June 1807, when he entered into an alliance with Russia, marked the height of Napoleon's power. The Empire would continue to expand, would win new wars, but victories would be each time more difficult to achieve and conquests each time a little more precarious.

To the north, Holland had become a kingdom under Louis Bonaparte, the father of the future Napoleon III. Belgium and Flanders were benefiting from the fast economic development of the country and from the Continental System which prevented competition with British products.

To the east, the Rhine was no longer the border: it had been pushed back to the river Elbe. Germany was under the control of vassal princes in Bavaria, Westphalia (given to Jérôme Bonaparte in 1807), Saxony, etc., and the Duchy of Poland acted as a buffer state with Russia.

To the south, French Italy saw, like Germany, its map simplified. Germany was arbitrarily divided into 15 departments, while the kingdom of Italy was composed of 24 departments with its capital in Milan, where a viceroy, Eugène de Beauharnais, was "reigning." The Kingdom of Naples, taken from the Bourbons who had sought refuge in Sicily, was under the authority of Joseph Bonaparte before passing on to Murat's one in 1808.

French laws, and above all the Civil Code, were enforced in all the States that had fallen under French influence. These new legal provisions helped obliterate the old regime while giving the Empire uniform administrative institutions.

Society was changing: nobility no longer dominated, but rather, notabilities. Merchants, lawyers, high-ranking officials, all belonging to a "propertied" bourgeoisie which was benefiting from the fast economic development, were gradually taking control of the machinery of power. The Code had been thought out for them and by them, whose main characteristic was to own land acquired during the Revolution. Public offices were reserved for them under the Constitution of Year VIII. The power of the bourgeoisie, still uncertain during the Revolution, would reach its height under the Consulate before weakening under the

imperial dictatorship. In the Year X (1802), only the highest taxpayers could be elected. The Empire saw the fast development of the administration and of its departments, and the creation of a full class of civil servants paid by the State. This phenomenon was detrimental to the working classes, peasants and labourers. The social mobility of the Revolution slowed down, then froze. Upward social mobility, which had become legendary in an army where *"every soldier was carrying a marshal's baton in his cartridge pouch"* in the days of the *"Fatherland in*

The triumphant entry of the Grande Armée into Paris through the Gate of Pantin, on November 25, 1807

Besides Great Britain, Russia remained the only enemy of the Empire. The victories at Eylau on February 6, 1807, then at Friedland on June 14, and the meeting at Tilsit which followed, led the French to think that, indoubtedly invincible, they had finally won... the peace. Here, Parisians acclaim Marshal Bessières leading the army. Nicolas-Antoine Taunay (1755-1830), Salon of 1810 Musée du château de Versailles.

danger" was no longer a reality. Privates were less and less likely to become officers.

At the same time, the imperial nobility, a caste close to the Emperor, comprised of marshals, high dignitaries and their families, was established. They first were endowed with titles and honors and granted as well riches brought by conquests.

As for the people, they were under close watch. Under the permanent threat of conscription, they had to beware of Fouché's agents who controlled at least the large cities, of gendarmes and of the secret police.

The state prisons, like the one at Vincennes, had been reopened to hold suspects sentenced by order of the Emperor.

An adventurer in the Revolution, but the heir to the capetian State more than to the men of 1789, Napoleon Bonaparte was reigning supreme over the most powerful country in Europe. Only England was still resisting, daring to stand up to him in the trial of strength initiated by the Continental System. The political mistakes made after 1807 would stem from the absolute necessity of perfecting that System.

After Tilsit: 1808-1812

The Logic of expansion

Like other vast empires, Napoleon's one was doomed to conquer or perish. Its creation was too recent to assure a real cohesion between the different nations it was comprised of, and its allies, freshly defeated, could turn against it at the first sign of weakness.

The Continental System was the symbol of the struggle against England and defined the opposite camps. No neutrality could be tolerated; when, in 1810, the Czar resumed relations with Great Britain to save his own economy from bankruptcy, Napoleon realized that he had one more potential enemy.

The Emperor of the French had started to lose his sharp sense of reality upon his return from Tilsit. Everything was obeying him, everything was going his way. Even the English were acting against they own interests and trying to intimidate Denmark by burning down Copenhagen, which led the Danes to close their ports to England in retaliation. Austria and Prussia, integrated into the Napoleonic system, had to break off diplomatic ties with London.

A small country however was ignoring the Continental System, which would cause its fall: Portugal, allied with England by centuries of political and commercial ties. Napoleon threatened to annex the troublemaker which was breaking the blockade. Spain authorized the passage of French troops across its territory, and even sent along its own troops. Junot crossed the Pyrenees, linked up with the Spanish, and broke up Portugal in 1807.

Pius VII too, who was willing to remain strictly neutral, was quickly despoiled of his States, before being arrested on July 6, 1809.

"There, it is not a case of extending our territory, assured Napoleon, it is prudence."

The history of the Empire could be summed up by the old saying *"Si vis pacem, para bellum"* (if you wish to have peace, prepare for war): it is difficult to tell if the wars waged by the Emperor were purely defensive or if Napoleon was merely forestalling the enemy. Driven by this complex dialectic, Napoleon could not but think about intervening in Spain on the first occasion. Reports sent to him on the domestic affairs of that country could not but convince him it would fall into his hands like a ripe fruit.

Spain was on the decline in 1808. Its grand colonial era, begun in the 16th century, had come to an end some twenty years before. Its king was Charles IV, a Bourbon and a descendant of Louis XIV's grandson, Philippe V. He passionately loved hunting, so much so that the real power resided with the queen, Marie-Louise de Parme, and the prime minister Godoy (who had also more intimate duties vis-à-vis the queen.)

The minister had had conferred on himself the title of "Prince of Peace" after the signing, in 1795, of the Peace of Basle, which ended the war between Spain and revolutionary France. Afterwards, he directed Spanish foreign policy towards a rapprochement with France. The San Ildefonso Agreement had confirmed that alliance.

That strategy allowed Godoy to invade Portugal with the blessing of Napoleon, who was then First Consul. But the Spanish economy had suffered a great deal from the war, which had caused a long interruption in its trade with its colonies. The breaking off of the Treaty of Amiens, in the spring of 1803, led Godoy to seek a genuine neutrality between France and England. Napoleon put his foot down, and a frightened Charles IV consented to loan his fleet. Most of that fleet was lost at Trafalgar in 1805. The English victory, which dealt a fatal blow to the French and Spanish navies, convinced Godoy that the Emperor of the French was heading for disaster. He was showing a far too advanced political foresight. The negotiations begun by the minister with the British were cut off abruptly after Jena, and Spain would remain a resigned, if not faithful, ally of the Emperor.

The Bourbons of Spain had the distinctive feature of hating each other. The queen, who was lending her full support to her lover Godoy, wanted to disinherit her eldest son, the future Ferdinand VII, who himself was asking the French to help him depose his father, Charles IV, who at the same time was also requesting them to subdue the prince. Napoleon was at first hesitant but, encouraged by Talleyrand who had by then already started to distanciate himself

The French army crossing the gorges of the Sierra de Guadarrama in December 1808

It is not solely the necessity to enforce the Continental System that led the Emperor to intervene in Spain. The spanish "hornet's nest" was, in fact, Napoleon's first strategic error. This conquest was being made for the Bonaparte dynasty. Napoleon intervened personally in Spain: he left Paris on October 29, and recapture Madrid, where he implemented various reforms, on December 4. But, in spite of the english threat to his lines of communication, he had to return to Paris, in view of Austria's sabre rattling. The Spanish affair was going to dramatically founder. Nicolas Antoine Taunay, Salon of 1812. Musée du château de Versailles.

from the Emperor, he made the mistake to intervene in order to ensure that the whole peninsula would respect the Continental System.

As the Bourbons had seemingly made peace, the Emperor decided to reinforce his troops which were already on the other side of the Pyrénées. Aware of the threat, Charles IV and his family considered fleeing to their possessions in South America, where they would be out of reach of the French.

The Spanish people, alarmed by rumors of their departure, put the blame on Godoy, who held the position of prime minister. The King of Spain dismissed his minister to pacify people, but that uprising against the queen's favorite was but the result of a deeper concern. Godoy miraculously escaped death in the midst of a turmoil which was getting out of hand. Charles IV felt that his abdication had become necessary, and prepared to hand over power to his son Ferdinand VII.

Murat, who was already marching on Madrid, quickened his pace and refused to recognize Ferdinand VII. The situation was extremely confused. Napoleon was trying to legitimize his presence in Spain by compelling the Bourbons to cede him their rights to the Crown. He proposed to Ferdinand VII that they meet in order to discuss the matter. The prince set off, anxious to defend his rights to the throne and ready, if necessary, to ally himself with the Emperor.

That move was neither to Charles IV's nor to the queen's liking; fearing that Napoleon would prefer their son to them, they went to Bayonne with Godoy to meet both Ferdinand VII and Napoleon. It was a painful scene; after repudiating his son, the old king, completely manipulated by Napoleon, agreed to reconsider his abdication and to name Murat as his lieutenant general.

Spain appeared to be conquered.

No attention however had been paid to the Spanish people.

Riding high on his previous successes, the Emperor had seriously underestimated the loyalty of the Spanish people to their monarchy, however decadent it was. He had also overlooked the religious element, intimately linked to the Spanish House of Bourbon. These errors of judgment doomed the Spanish venture from the beginning. The need to defend itself against the French aggression brought to life in Spain a religious "fundamentalism" all the more dangerous since it combined the political and the spiritual. The Spanish people were soon no longer fighting against occupying forces, but against heretics. The war had become a crusade.

Neither the need to "regenerate" that country nor the necessity to strictly enforce the Continental

System alone led Napoleon to intervene in Spain. The Spanish "hornet's nest" was the Emperor's first blunder, the first truly "imperial" war which had been waged for personal reasons. This conquest was being made in the name of France for the House of Bonaparte, and public opinion could hardly accept it.

Napoleon visiting Les Invalides hospital, on February 11, 1808

The carnage of the Battle of Eylau in February 1807 had genuinely moved the Emperor. The war in Spain was going to reveal the atrocities of guerrilla warfare. Times when sufferings were endured in the name of the fatherland or for glory's sake would become a thing of the past.
Alexandre Veron-Bellecourt (1773-circa 1840),
Salon of 1812.
Musée du château de Versailles.

Napoleon, speaking of the Bourbons, once confided to Metternich:

"They are my personal enemies; both of us cannot sit on thrones in Europe at the same time."

Alexander I would not say otherwise in 1813. The intervention in Spain could be justified by many legitimate arguments: the hesitant diplomacy of Godoy, who nearly betrayed France and was brought back on the right track by the victory at Jena, was unequivocal. As Spain was not a reliable ally and its rulers were unable to govern, there was no alternative but to integrate it into the Napoleonic order.

But why depose Charles IV? Why eliminate Ferdinand VII by sending him into a gilded exile to Talleyrand's estate in Valençay? Napoleon did not know how to come to terms with Time; he was eager to build, in a few years, a european order capable of replacing the structure which prevailed until 1789, and had taken several centuries to be established. Continuing the dream of Louis XIV and forgetting the vicissitudes of the War of Succession, he had decided to put one of his brothers on the Spanish throne, turning the former country of Charles V into a "family" property.

That was, without doubt, the cause of his failure in Spain.

On May 2, 1808 *(Dos de Mayo)*, Madrid rose up against the French, and massacred all isolated individuals. Napoleon showed his true colours and returned blow for blow: to rule Spain through a puppet king had become irrelevant. A terrorized Charles IV abdicated unconditionally in favour of the Emperor. Murat had managed meanwhile to reestablish order. Napoleon sent him to rule Naples, while Joseph was given Spain. It was more of a curse than a blessing.

The rebellion spread soon to the whole country; inflamed by the clergy who was advocating a crusade against the "Antichrist," rich and poor rose up against the French conquerors. Trained by soldiers of the former Spanish army, peasants and craftsmen learnt how to handle weapons. Following Madrid, big cities such as Oviedo or Saragossa rose up, followed soon afterwards by entire provinces (Galicia, Catalonia). The resistance, instigated and supported by the English, formed a national junta, based first in Seville, then in Cadiz. The war would last a long time, compelling Napoleon to send there troops he would sorely need later.

The insurrection spread then to Portugal where Arthur Wellesley, the future Duke of Wellington, had just landed. The war was taking a new turn, entirely different from the previous conflicts; disciplined and seasoned troops were helpless against the explosion of hatred of a population exasperated by the conqueror's misdeeds. Junot was overrun by a population in arms and had to surrender to the English. At Baylen and at Vimeiro, the French armies were beaten by Spanish

patriots or by the English. Portugal had to be entirely evacuated, while news of the French setbacks was raising Napoleon's foes' hopes and ending the myth of the invincibility of his soldiers. The blow dealt to the Empire, both tactically and to its supporters' morale, was considerable. Even the Emperor's allies, for the most part opposed to the return of the Bourbons, began to doubt. Aware of his loss of prestige, Napoleon flew into a rage, and promised:

"Spain will be reconquered in autumn!"
But before autumn, there would be Erfurt.

Erfurt, "swarming with kings," where Talleyrand began to betray his former accomplice of Brumaire.

"The Rhine, the Alps and the Pyrenees have been conquered by France, the imperial dignitary was telling the Czar, all the rest has been conquered by Napoleon, conquests France does not support..."

Fouché had come closer to the former Minister of Foreign Affairs who had become Grand Chamberlain. Both were worried by the expansion of the Empire. Working closely every day with their master, they had understood that nothing could stop his ravenous hunger for new conquests. His despotism and his intervention in Spain which was only justified —besides the blockade— by the annexation of another crown to the House of Bonaparte, were rousing the resentment of public opinion.

Napoleon needed to withdraw the Grande Armée from Germany for his Spanish campaign, but he did not trust Austria enough to leave it unguarded. He had thought that his "dear" Russian ally could fulfill that duty, and had wanted to meet him to reassert their understanding. The meeting had been devised as another opportunity to restate the French authority in Germany.

The Franco-Russian honeymoon had been weakened by a few insolvable disputes, the most serious being Constantinople, which above all Napoleon did not want to give to the Czar in any future carving of the Ottoman Empire. A joint military expedition, planned for the spring of 1808, had been postponed because of the Spanish affair. An impatient Czar was resolutely waiting for his ally to renew his offers. The war in Spain was, in a way, the cause of Napoleon's break-up with Alexander.

By diverting the Emperor from his eastern conquests, that war was deeply disappointing the Czar and leading him to disassociate himself from the fate of his French ally.

The stumbling block of Constantinople was additionally showing to the two parties that there was one too many of them in Europe, stirring up a veiled hostility between them. No one, however, wanted war in 1808: Napoleon because he was bogged down in Spain, and Alexander because he was convinced of the solidity of the might of his rival.

Talleyrand changed the Czar's plans at Erfurt, opening his eyes and cleverly painting in glowing colours the part of "liberator" of Europe, he would become so impassioned with. The Emperor arrived in Erfurt at the end of September, relying on his charm to seduce Alexander and on Talleyrand to take care of his ministers. But Alexander, who was not as well-disposed as at Tilsit (circumstances had changed), did not fall under Napoleon's spell as the year before. In agreement with Metternich, the Austrian, Talleyrand was making sure to destroy in the evening the work done by Napoleon during the day.

Spurred by the former bishop of Autun, the Czar refused to be the "watchdog" of Austria, and, all smiles, began to dream of a future without Napoleon. Knowing it could count on Russian neutrality, Vienna could prepare for war in order to go on the offensive in the spring of 1809.

Leaving Erfurt after that diplomatic defeat, Napoleon knew he could expect to have to fight soon on the Danube. Everything would depend on the speed of the operations in Spain. The Emperor left Paris on October 29, and recaptured Madrid on December 4, after jostling the Spanish at Somosierra. In order to attract the support of the liberals and of the classes formerly proFrench, Napoleon undertook to carry out a few reforms: he abolished the Inquisition, feudal rights and a third of the convents... It had been a quick campaign but less brilliant than the previous ones: the troop's morale was low, and there were several cases of insubordination; rivalries between military commanders had allowed the enemy to escape nearly unscathed.

Napoleon surrounded by his family on the terrace of the palace at St Cloud, in 1810

Napoleon wanted an heir that he could not hope to have with Joséphine. He has just received the hand of Marie-Louise, daughter of Francis I of Austria. The hopes for his dynasty take shape.
Louis Ducis (1775-1847), Salon of 1810.
Musée du château de Versailles.

On December 19, Napoleon learnt that the English threatened to cut off the road from Madrid to Burgos, that is its communication lines with France. He set off to surprise them, but after being informed of Austria's war preparations, he had to go back to Paris entrusting the command of his troops to Marshal Soult.

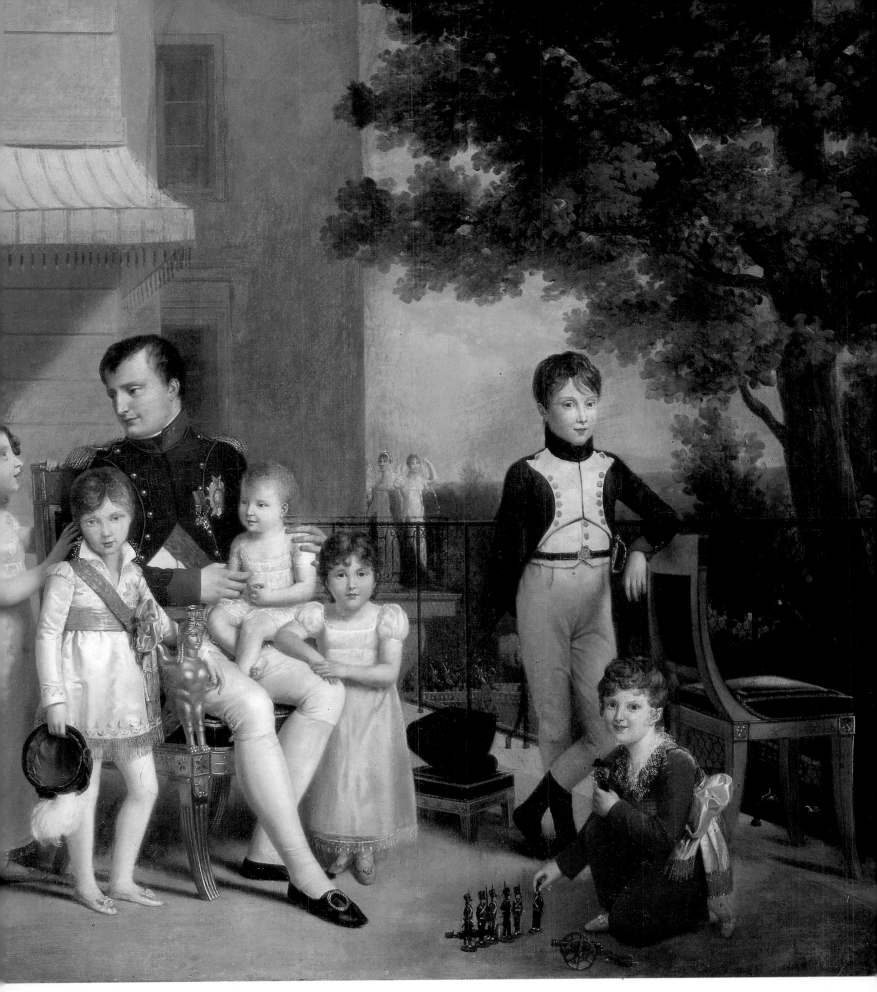

Other disquieting rumors were justifying his return: as on the eve of Marengo, Talleyrand and Fouché had "prepared" his possible succession by sounding out Murat. Napoleon vowed to bring them to heel.

The Spanish affair, which could not be "settled" on time, would got bogged down and would have catastrophic consequences on the fate of the Empire. The rebellious provinces would keep on trading with England, while the Spanish colonies in America would open up to its products. A lampoon of the time was stating ironically that the blockade could have been effective *"if at the same time the French government was taking so violent measures to close the European*

The Prince Klemens Wenzel Nepomuk Lothar von Metternich

Born in Coblenz on May 15, 1771, his first influences were from his mother, who was close to the grand empress Marie-Thérèse. He received the best French education and as a student in Strasbourg, witnessed the turbulent events of the Revolution. He believed in Napoleon's invincibility up until he read the 29th Bulletin of the Grand Army, which acknowledged the disastrous retreat from Russia. He wanted to place Austria in the role of mediator in a future peace based on compromise, but later decided to switch from this position of armed neutrality to that of partner in the European Coalition against Napoleon. From a count, he was made prince after the allied victory at Leipzig. He always held mixed feelings of hatred and admiration for Napoleon.

Next pages
Marie-Louise and Napoleon the Great

With this union, Napoleon became the nephew of Louis XVI by marriage. The Hapsburg monarchy seemed to be a source of support not insignificant for the edifice Napoleon had built.It gave Austria, on the other hand,the years necessary to return to the forefront. Ambiguity reigned.

markets to the British Isles, it had not taken even more violent ones to open to them the markets of Latin America."

The Emperor's return to Paris on January 23, 1809, is remembered for the famous scene a few days later on the 28th where he lashes out against Talleyrand:

"You are a thief, a coward, a man of no faith. You don't believe in God, you have betrayed everyone, nothing is sacred to you [...]. Why, you are just shit in silk stockings!"

Talleyrand offered a cool indifference to that rather justified overall desciption of himself, and merely concluded with a sigh:

"What a pity such a great man was so badly brought up!"

Napoleon made then a fatal mistake: instead of getting rid of that accomplice who betrayed him, he only discharged him of his responsibility of Vice-Grand Elector (*"the only vice that he is lacking,"* according to our dear Fouché...). That strange attitude would last until 1814: as he considered Talleyrand indispensable to the smooth running of his affairs, the Emperor would insult and humiliate him without ever resolving to have him shot for high treason. His generosity was indeed misplaced: Talleyrand would one day sign the treaty putting an end to the Empire...

Meanwhile, and until that twilight, Napoleon had to resolve to go and fight Austria which, in spite of the Emperor's warnings, thought its time has come. The Emperor's position was in fact rather precarious, with his best troops bogged down in Spain, Germany grumbling under the yoke, and Russia confining itself to a more or less hostile neutrality. Napoleon was to play double or quits for the fourth time.

Archduke Charles invaded Bavaria on April 10, 1809. On the 17th, Napoleon was in Donauwerth and was galvanizing his men who appeared momentarily lost. The Grande Armée was then mostly made up of new conscripts who had never fought and needed to be trained before even thinking of fighting the decisive battle. Archduke Charles, who had hoped to separately defeat Davout and Masséna, had to beat a retreat in Bohemia after his rout in Eckmühl.

Bad news were coming from everywhere else. The Austrians had jostled Prince Eugène in Italy and taken Warsaw without upsetting the Czar; Tyrol has risen up, and Germany was rumbling. England was not sitting passively: Wellington recaptured Porto and drove Soult out of Galicia in May, while on July 29, an expeditionary force was landing —without result— on Walcheren Island in Holland. Fouché's action, in mobilizing energies and organizing defense, was decisive; but the Emperor took offense at having been "replaced" by his police minister, and dismissed him soon after.

Meanwhile, Napoleon had set up camp in Schönbrunn on May 10. Vienna surrendered on the 13th. A few days later, Lanne was mortally wounded at Essling and the French had to cross back the Danube. The Battle of Wagram, won on July 6, determined in the end the fate of the campaign. The victor, preoccupied with the Spanish affairs and the far too ambiguous attitude of Russia, could hardly refuse the Austrian peace proposals.

The war of "destruction" promised to Austria by Napoleon would end in a marriage. In Erfurt, Alexander had remained vague about the possibility of a dynastic union between France and Russia. Yet it was vital for Napoleon to have an heir and Joséphine, in spite of all her efforts, had now proven to be desperately sterile.

A character would then take center-stage diplomatically: Metternich. This prince, of Rhenish origin, was educated in Saxony and in Berlin, then sent to Paris in 1806 as the Austrian ambassador. He had been able to meet Napoleon, to talk to him and to size up accurately his personality and psychology during three years. These were trump cards in the perilous game Austria had to play.

Metternich very quickly understood he could turn the Emperor's wish to remarry to his advantage. A union with one of the daughters of Francis I, Archduchess Marie-Louise, would prevent an always possible strengthening of the alliance between Napoleon and Alexander. Alexander declined a formal offer for the hand of his sister. The same day, on January 7, 1810, Marie-Louise was given to the "Ogre of Corsica."

K. Garnier

89

MARIE LOUISE,

*Impératrice des Français, Reine d'Italie,
et protectrice de la Société maternelle de l'Empire.*

NAPOLÉON LE GRAND,

Empereur des Français, Roi d'Italie
et protecteur de la Confédération du Rhin &.

It was a deft sacrifice for Austria which thus won the few years of respite needed for its recovery, while widening the rift between between Paris and St Petersburg. The treaty signed with France, which deprived it of Illyria and part of Galicia, and forced it to halve its army could only be temporary. The Habsburg knew that he would resume fighting sooner or later, when the Russian eagle had decided to lend its support. In the meantime, the Austrian policy appear staunchly pro-French to put everyone off the track.

As for Napoleon, he was joining the restricted circle of European reigning families... and was becoming King Louis XVI's nephew by marriage, which worried the French people amazed to see their monarch take up again with the Ancien Régime, twenty years after the fall of the Bastille. But had not Napoleon, the crowned heir of the Revolution, been betraying it since the end of the Consulate?

That policy of "reversal of alliances," inaugurated by Louis XV in the middle of the 18th century, still appeared to be the best one to follow in the perilous situation the Empire was. During the campaign of 1809, the master of Europe had been able to realize how strong and above all politically stable Austria was. In the shifting world of alliances reluctantly entered into and of people subdued by the force of arms, the Habsburg monarchy appeared to be a rather significant support to the napoleonic Empire.

The birth of the "Eaglet," on March 10, 1811, reinforced the continuity of the dynasty. The child was given immediately the title of "King of Rome," in reference to the title of "King of Romans" formerly conferred to the heir to the Holy Roman Empire. Napoleon's vainglory was at its peak; his brothers and sisters were ruling Europe and the Emperor manipulated them like puppets. He purely and simply took away the kingdom of Holland from Louis, who was turning more Dutch than French, and deprived as well Joseph of the northern provinces of Spain. Nothing could seemingly resist the will of the Emperor. Even proud England, struck by an unprecedented economic crisis, was on the verge of ruin in 1811. Napoleon's Empire was no longer French only. Napoleon was already thinking of ruling over a confederation of European states united under one same scepter: his own.

A danger however was threatening that dream: Russia, which could not conceal its hostility any more. Tilsit had been Alexander's doing, but he had not been followed by the Russian high society who was more anglophile than the Czar. As time went by, he had grown offended to be constantly confined to the second position in Europe. Napoleon was overshadowing him, and he could not stand it. Talleyrand's advice, in Erfurt, had proven to him that his rival's authority was not as steady as he had thought. Then, the dispute over Constantinople continued to weigh heavily on the relations between the two emperors. Alexander eventually convinced himself that any agreement signed with Napoleon would turn to his disadvantage. It meant embarking on a course that will inevitably lead to war.

The Czar was no fool and was careful not to challenge France openly. Nevertheless, his behaviour during the campaign of 1809 and his increasingly lax support of the Continental System had quickly caused an obvious chilling of the relations between Paris and St Petersburg. As with Talleyrand, and in spite of these troubling signs, Napoleon remained captive to the friendship he felt for the Czar since Tilsit. He sincerely believed that their mutual friendship was such that an agreement was still possible.

At the beginning of 1812, finally aware of the deteriorating situation, the Emperor worked towards establishing alliances with war in his mind. While Turkey and Sweden obstinately refused, Prussia and Austria accepted to follow him whether they liked it or not. But the commitment of these two "allies" would be timid enough to be useless to the Grande Armée. Although he was a signatory of the treaty of March 1812, binding Austria and France, Metternich made sure to let the Czar know how well-disposed he felt towards him.

In order to keep Alexander at bay and to compel him to rethink his foreign policy, Napoleon assembled in Germany an army of nearly 700,000 men, half of which only were French. On April 25, 1812, the Czar sent an ultimatum to his old "friend" from Tilsit. Forced to wage a war he did not really want, the Emperor crossed the Niemen on June 24 at the head of his armies. He may have sincerely hoped it would be the last one. And indeed, the ashes of Moscow were his last conquest.

The King of Rome

Born on March 20 1811, the infant was given immediately the title of "King of Rome." Napoleon's dynasty appeared to be saved.
Sketch by Jean-Baptiste Isabey (1767-1855), dated 1811.

MARS 1811

J. Isabey. 1811

The weaknesses of the napoleonic "system"

As Napoleon was penetrating deep into the Russian steppes, his vast Empire has only two years left to live. Why was this "colossus with feet of clay" so fragile in fact, and so dependent on the military successes of its master?

Many cracks had appeared in the structure both inside and outside. We saw that dignitaries such as Talleyrand had not hesitated to lapse into betrayal as early as 1808 (and perhaps even 1807); Fouché had made himself indispensable, but he was serving the police state of his dreams more than Napoleon. Enriched by their earlier campaigns, gorged with titles and satiated with honours, the young officers of the Campaign of Italy turned marshals of the Empire were longing to enjoy peacefully their old age. All these men who had so powerfully contributed to the creation of that "napoleonic" Europe with their energy and ambition had lost the taste for adventure. Napoleon himself felt he was physically declining, less ready to make the lightning decisions that served his genius so much, less resistant to the fatigues oof war.

The heroes had become gouty.

The populations under the French yoke, and the French themselves, were tired of the perpetual and bloody conflicts in which all their young people were slaughtered. There was an increasing number of draft evaders, who were enjoying a strong support in their villages or their native regions. The economy was running out of steam, seized up by the side effects of the Continental System which had paralyzed trade shipping routes. Taxes, too heavy because of the successive military campaigns, were being increasingly rejected by a bourgeoisie deprived of the political role it had aspired to under the Revolution. Paying dearly for a glory that had brought them nothing in return, the elite of the "notabilities" was only talking of making peace with the enemies of France who, in its words, were rather the enemies of the Emperor.

Poorly handled, the conflict with the Papacy had taken a turn detrimental to Napoleon's interests. The imprisonment of Pius VII in Savona symbolized the repressive nature of the imperial regime and underscored the deep rift between the Emperor and the faithful. The spirit of the Concordat of 1801, which had been the foundations of Napoleon's grandeur, was dead and prompting the crumbling of these very foundations.

The Emperor's entourage itself was a ferment of fragility for the imperial regime. Apart for the ministers, who were only administrators subservient to the monarch's views and without political opinions of their own, the new imperial nobility was reminding too much the old revolutionaries of 1789 of the former one. The most well-known names of the former monarchy were mingling with those of dignitaries of common birth, forming a privileged caste which had learnt nothing from the past terrible years.

Foreign events were worrisome. Spain had been keeping on devouring the best troops of the Grande Armée for the last three years. The "hornet's nest" was fully working militarily and above all psychologically, in favour of the English and of Napoleon's foes. The success of the guerrilla war, supported by Wellington, raised high hopes in other countries eager to regain their liberty, and particularly in Germany.

Behind the scenes Prussia and its satellite principalities were plotting a general insurrection. Austria had given one of its archduchesses to avoid giving itself, and was following a complex policy, made of short-lived protestations of friendship and long term damaging betrayals.

The Continental System, which nearly brought England to her knees, had been broken by Alexander at the end of December 1810. Napoleon had lost his biggest battle, the one most costly in men and efforts: now England would never yield. The various restrictions which were weighing on the national economies had therefore become useless, and the destruction of the Empire would be soon considered as a necessary and vital fight.

From unpopular, Napoleon and his "system" became hated. The invasion of Russia was a forward retreat, the last grand bet of the napoleonic adventure. If he were victorious, the Emperor would force Russia to restore the Continental System and a strangled England would have to evacuate Spain. If he were defeated, he would have to relinquish the initiative to his enemies. On June 24, 1812, Napoleon crossed the Niemen as Caesar once crossed the Rubicon. But the glorious sun of Austerlitz would be replaced by the pale and icy one of the Russian winter.

Napoleon's white piqué frock coat

The Emperor's classic gray frock coat came in various shapes and colours. Pictured here is a white frock coat, the ghostly look of which eerily makes one think of a shroud, the one of the dreadful retreat from Russia, where so many men perished in the frozen steppes.
Musée de la Malmaison.

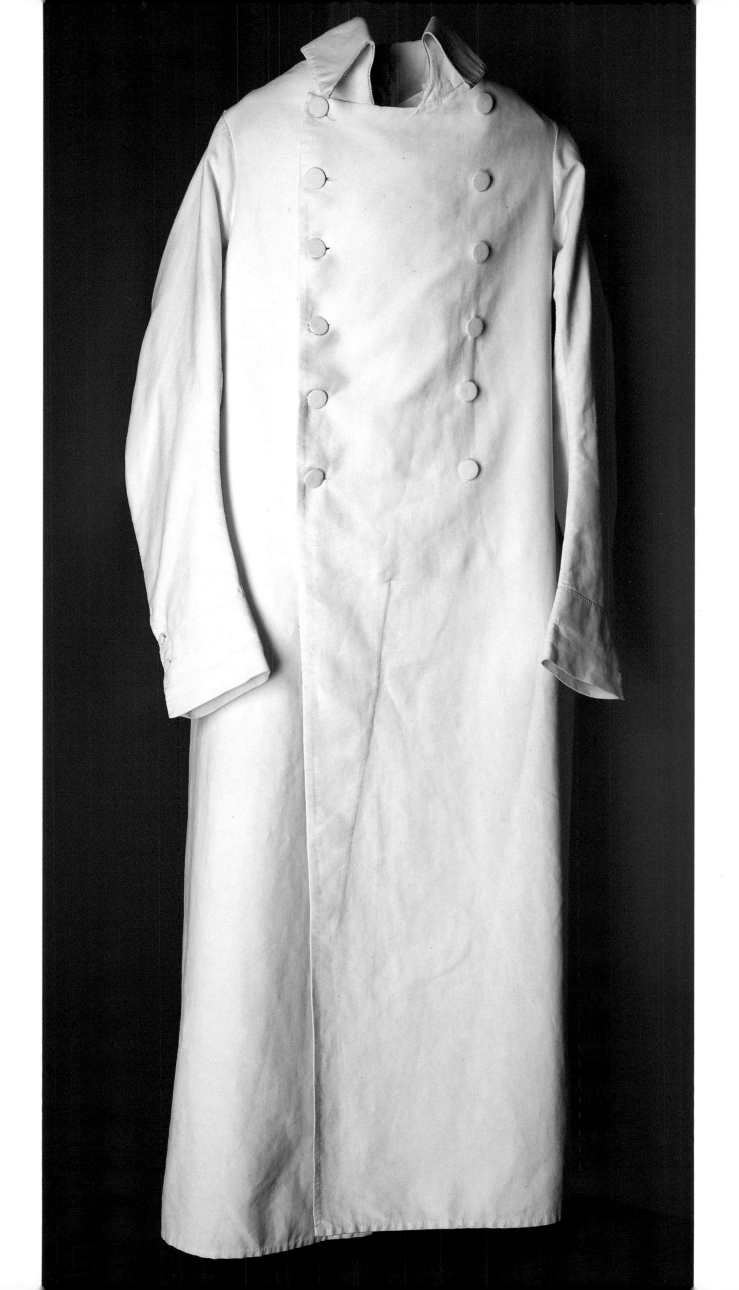

The end of the Epic times: 1812-1815

The initial setbacks: 1812-1813

The Campaign of Russia: 1812

The Grande Armée had lost a month to assemble in Germany before it could go on the offensive. It will badly miss these few weeks afterwards.

Napoleon's objective, when entering Russia, was certainly not to annihilate it, but to compel the Czar to negotiate with him after having dealt him a quick and decisive defeat. As the campaign was expected to end in the fall, there was theoretically nothing to be feared from the Russian winter.

But Alexander withdrew. He knew pretty well that his forces were greatly inferior to the invaders' ones and that his finest generals, Bennigson and Kutusov, were momentarily removed from command. The vastness of his country and the obstinacy with which Russians would defend their land were his strength. In many ways the national consciousness of modern Russia was forged in 1812. Its inhabitants found themselves united against Napoleon's armies and fought against them, under the distant aegis of the Czar.

As he knew he was a very poor strategist, the Czar had enough sense to stay and worry in St Petersburg, while his generals were at work. He had indeed contemplated at the beginning of the campaign to take command of his troops, but their defiant reaction quickly dissuaded him to do so.

Napoleon was bewildered by the lack of resistance from the Russians, who allowed him to enter Vilna without a fight. General Balachov joined him while he was setting up his quarters there, in order to spy on him and sound him out. Alexander's emissary asserted that there was still time to negotiate if the Emperor was crossing back the Nieman with all his men.

Napoleon could not afford to back off in this manner: his prestige would have been seriously undermined and vassal countries, kept in subjection with great difficulty, would have taken an opportunity to rise up. The conqueror proposed to negotiate on acceptable terms: would not Alexander agree to help him against the English as he did at Tilsit?

Balachov did not reply. And as Napoleon was asking him the way to Moscow, the ambassador loftily retorted:

"Sire, you may go by whichever route you like best to Moscow. Charles XII went by way of Poltava."

It as an allusion to Peter the Great's victory over the king of Sweden, a century before...

Two more weeks were lost in Vilna to assemble the huge army scattered throughout the steppe. There were already many deserters. When it reached Vitebsk at the end of July, the Grande Armée had 150,000 men less, most of whom either got lost, fell sick, or deserted, as the rare fights had been but skirmishes very limited in scope.

Napoleon, who could not retreat, was lured inland by the flight of the Russian generals. Their strategy was clear: they wanted to entice him away from his bases so as to starve his troops, and fight them only after they had been exhausted by famine and by marches. Even if the "resistance party's" influence was growing within the Russian ruling circles as the invader was coming closer to Moscow, the partisans of the "scorched-earth" policy were still a majority. And the Emperor was sadly stating:

"The very danger pushes us on to Moscow! The wise men have run out of objections..."

The Russian generals finally decided to face Napoleon in order to protect Moscow. The two armies clashed at Borodino where Kutusov, the new commander-in-chief, was solidly entrenched. The French welcomed with relief the opportunity to fight: anything but this perpetual flight onwards!

The battle of Borodino, or of the Moskova, took place on September 7, 1812. Napoleon, sick and more worried than ever, did not show his usual genius; the Grande Armée remained in control of the battlefield through heavy losses only. The road to Moscow was opened, but Kutusov had been able to manage an orderly withdrawal and his forces were still considerable.

On September 14, the French entered Moscow.

Napoleon was to stay on one month in the Russian city, three-quarters of which had been burnt down by order of Governor Rostopchine. He was waiting for Alexander to oblige him by replying to the peace proposal he had sent him. But the Czar, outraged and in the grip of another mystical crisis, was refusing to start negotiations with the "Antichrist."

"One of us must disappear from the world scene" he stated.

On October 19, worried by the onset of winter and afraid of finding himself isolated in the immensity of the steppe, the Emperor left Moscow to return to his starting point.

The capture of the great Russian city allowed him to save face in the eyes of his subjects, even if the outcome was questionable in strategic terms. Kutusov manoeuvred then to compel the French to take back the same route they came by, the Smolensk road already devastated by their passage.

Encumbered with their loot, without either food or clothes which could help them withstand the intense cold, the soldiers of the Grande Armée were forced to retrace their steps, harried by the Cossacks and the russian peasants. Napoleon received at that moment news of the conspiracy of General Malet, who nearly seized power by spreading rumours of his death. The Emperor could assess with awe the fragility of his power, and the possible political consequences of the russian disaster. The crossing of the Berezina river on November 27, 28 and 29, marked the final catastrophe of that campaign.

On December 3, in Molodetchna, was published the 29th Bulletin of the Grande Armée in which Napoleon admitted being the victim of an "atrocious calamity." As he foresaw the commotion the announcement would cause throughout the empire, he resigned himself to abandon his men to their sad fate to return as quickly as possible to Paris in order to bolster his faltering power. Hence the incredible sleigh-ride home in the company of Caulaincourt.

When they crossed into Prussian territory, Napoleon hid on the bottom of the sleigh for fear of being recognized and taken prisoner. On December 18, both made it at last to the Tuileries, exhausted, filthy, unrecognizable but safe and sound. The vanquished conqueror, the fugitive from Germany was once again the master of Europe. But for how long?

The defeat had been disastrous in terms of prestige, of men and of equipment. The empire had lost in a few months the biggest part of its offensive forces. Other armies would be raised, other battles fought, but the Emperor would always be short of something to turn ordinary victories into enemy routs. The campaign of Germany would be severely affected by the lack of cavalry and a shortage of artillery.

Seemingly at least, nothing was really lost at the end of December 1812. The imperial possessions had not suffered from the war, and the Emperor's authority remained in principle undisputed from the Pyrenees to the Elbe. Spain and Portugal were still restless but Wellington's troops were unable to secure a decisive advantage.

Aside from Prussia, Napoleon dominated the whole of Germany thanks to his alliances and fortresses; Austria was bound to France by a dynastic tie she would certainly not breach willingly.

"I have made a serious mistake," the Emperor was telling his ministers, *"but I can correct it."*

A new army was raised to fully replace the one lost in Russia. To these fresh, but not very seasoned troops, theoretically 650,000 in number, Alexander could only oppose soldiers exhausted by the campaign which just ended, commanded by generals reluctant to venture beyond their borders and not sharing the Czar's mystical vision of his mission of "liberator of Europe."

England was still too weak to support Alexander apart for its "subsidies." Furthermore a war against the United States was compelling her to send across the Atlantic troops which could have been valuable in Spain. The burden of war would be entirely shouldered by Russia, should she decide to pursue her advantage by marching west.

The campaign of Germany and the attitude of Austria would decide the fate of Europe.

Next pages
The Battle of the Moskova, on September 7, 1812, the second attack on the grand redoubt

After fleeing right to the gates of Moscow, the Russian generals were eventually forced to confront the Emperor. The two armies clashed at Borodino where Koutousov, was solidly entrenched. The fight was on at last. A sick Napoleon, only succeeded in controlling the battlefield through the sacrifice of heavy losses and, though the road to Moscow was open, the Russians had been able to effect an orderly withdrawal. The war was by no means over yet. Baron Louis-Francois Lejeune (1775 - 1848), dated 1822, Salon of 1824. Musée du château de Versailles.

The Campaign of Germany: 1813

The first act of that campaign was the defection of the Prussian General Yorck, who went over to the service of the Czar by the Convention of Tauroggen on December 30, 1812. Although it was officially a personal decision, he was in fact acting under the verbal instructions of Frederick William III of Prussia. This shy and submissive king was striving to have a foot in each camp.

His pledges of loyalty to Napoleon quickly got lost in the immense turmoil of the German "War of liberation" inspired by thinkers and politicians such as Fichte, Gneisenau, Hardenberg or Baron Stein. Realizing moreover that the remains of the Grande Armée could not resist the flood of Russian troops, Frederick William started discussions with the Czar to negotiate officially his defection.

Alexander knew exactly the difficult position of the Prussian monarch and imposed his own terms by threatening to deprive him of his throne. By signing the treaty of Kalish, on February 27, 1813, the king of Prussia was tying his fate to the Russian armies' one and going to war against Napoleon. One of the points of that treaty concerned the reconstitution of Poland under the Czar's authority, a more concrete motive for his hostility towards France than the part of "liberator" he wanted to play.

A month after Kalish, Kutusov was calling on all Germans to rise up against the French yoke.

At the end of April, Napoleon rejoined his new army at Erfurt. It numbered 145,000 men, whereas the Russian and Prussian forces could only muster 80,000. He had promised to *"pull on his italian boots"* and kept his word. In four battles, including Lützen and Bautzen, he repelled the allies and forced them back across the Elbe. Alexander and Frederick William lost faith in their lucky star, and especially the king of Prussia who was fearing for his capital city. Napoleon's prestige was such that it took very little to restore its former glory. And everyone knew that it was winter, and not the Russian troops, which had forced the disastrous retreat of the previous year.

The Emperor however had not been able to fully benefit from his successes due to a shortage of calvary. Losing himself confidence in his chances of victory, perhaps tired of a war which, being strictly defensive, did not bring him anything, he accepted Austria's "armed" mediation at the beginning of June. An armistice was signed at Pleswitz for a few weeks, allowing both sides to accumulate reserves of men and of equipment before returning to battle.

This diplomatic interlude was one of the highlights of Metternich's career. An ally of France, Austria did not consider betraying her at the beginning of 1813. Or had she had been thinking about it loud

The Battle of Lützen, on May 2, 1813.

On February 28, 1813, the king of Prussia allied himself with Russia. By the end of April, Napoleon took command of his new army at Erfurt. 145,000 strong against 80,000 Russians and Prussians, and led by an inspired Napoleon, that army forced the allies back across the Elbe after four battles, including the one at Lützen.

enough to be heard in St Petersburg, she did not do it. The Prussian participation in the war against the French was already sketching out a coalition which, if victorious, could be harsh against a country with dynastic ties to Napoleon. Hence the "armed" mediation, which allowed Austria to contact the Emperor's adversaries without (too much) vexing him, while mobilizing in order to have an army capable of intervening in the conflict. Metternich did not know which camp to join. He was eagerly awaiting

Napoleon's defeat, as were all Austrians since 1805 and 1809. The Habsburg empire however could not afford to make a third blunder. It was difficult to believe that the monarchy, which had avoided destruction after Wagram by sacrificing an archduchess, would survive a third defeat.

Metternich preferred to achieve these aims by peaceful means rather than by gambling on the fortunes of war. Posing as a mediator, he could impose his views on Napoleon while keeping the option, should Napoleon refuse, to defect honourably to the other camp. The fatal meeting took place in Dresden on June 26. The Emperor, who knew his Metternich, approached him rather abruptly: *"You want war? Well, you will have it. [...] I shall see you in Vienna."*

The Austrian having questioned the military worth of the young conscripts comprising the imperial army, Napoleon, according to him, would have let out:

"A man like me cares little about the lives of a million men [...] Your sovereigns born on the throne can let themselves be beaten twenty times and still return to their capital. I cannot do so, because I am an upstart soldier."

Before parting, the two men exchanged the final words of this memorable conversation:

"You will not wage war against me," said the Emperor, patting Metternich on the shoulder. He merely replied, icily: *"Sire, you are lost."*

Aware that he was not in a position to impose his will, Napoleon agreed to negotiate and accepted the principle of a conference in Prague.

These negotiations took place in a rather peculiar atmosphere. The Austrian army was waiting on a war footing to find out whether it should march on Paris or Berlin, while the English were asserting they would never sign a treaty which would not take into consideration their interests.

Then came the news that Wellington had crushed the French at Vittoria on June 21, 1813. The Spanish war was over, after five years of exhausting battles. Great Britain had cleverly used the peninsula to immobilize troops which would have been more useful elsewhere. That war, lost in advance because of insufficient forces and of negligent generals, had cost the empire dearly. The battle of Talavera, fought on July 28, 1809, and won by Wellington over Victor and Jourdan, had vindicated the relevance of the British policy. After besieging Ciudad Rodrigo, Masséna had attacked Lisbon with little success, and, had to beat a retreat after the inconclusive victory of Fuentes de Oñoro on May 3, 1811.

Determined to attack Russia, Napoleon was no more interested in the Spanish "hornet's nest." He just protected the Madrid-Bayonne corridor letting the English reconquer, slowly but surely, the rest of the country. Wellington was advancing and most of the

The Battle of Leipzig, on October 16, 1813.

On August 26 and 27, the Emperor crushed the main enemy formation before Dresden. But, having taken refuge with 200,000 men in Leipzig, he had to fight the Coalition army. "The Battle of Nations", as it is known, lasted three days; the Allies won, forcing the Emperor to retreat to the Rhine.
Colored engraving, property of Bernasconi et Co., n° 67, Grande Rue de la Guillotiere, Lyon.

French counter-attacks, which were but abrupt and inconsequential engagements, failed because of dissension between the French generals. On October 8, 1813, Wellington crossed the Bidassoa. The Spanish war was over.

The announcement of Wellington's final victory over the French in Spain, in addition to Napoleon's determination not to abandon any of his conquests, led to the failure of the Congress of Prague in the summer of 1813. Metternich had reached his objective: Napoleon was bearing the moral responsibility of the

war and not the Allies, whom Austria has joined forces with from then on. The second phase of the Campaign of Germany could begin. The balance of forces was in favour of the Allies, who had 860,000 men while the Emperor could only muster 700,000, after utilizing all his reserves.

The fortunes of war remained uncertain throughout the months of August and September. On August 27 and 28, the Emperor crushed the main enemy formation before Dresden, but a few days earlier Bülow had saved Berlin from Oudinot's army. On October 16, Napoleon, who had taken refuge with 200,000 men in Leipzig, had to fight the Coalition army. *"The Battle of Nations,"* as it is known, lasted three days and ended in an allied victory. The vanquished Emperor retreated to the Rhine to establish there his last line of defense… and to give the order to raise a new army for the Campaign of France. It would be the army of the "Marie-Louise," comprised of adolescents so nicknamed because of their extreme youth.

The Long Agony: 1814-1815

The Campaign of France: 1814

Victorious in Leipzig, the Allies were quite naturally divided over the next course of action: should they deal with or invade France? should not they fear that burst of popular fervour which had brought defeat in Valmy? The differences in their respective interests were beginning to poison their relationship.

The Prussians were quite simply asking for Napoleon's deposition, recommending to march all the way to Paris to break up France. Alexander was not against his foe's "deposition," but refused to be too hard on the defeated nation. As for the Cabinet in London, it was afraid of seeing the French stand up as one man should they dare lay a finger on their Emperor. The Austrians were very much wondering which course of action to follow, opting eventually for the accession of Napoleon II under the regency of Marie-Louise.

Nobody really wanted to cross the Rhine, apart from the Prussians and the Czar who was dreaming of avenging the affront made to Moscow. Peace proposals were sent to Napoleon from Frankfurt, where the leaders of the Coalition had gathered. The Emperor could not bring himself to abandon his conquests. He first answered in the negative to all the proposals made by the Allies, and agreed to them too late, when the military situation had turned to his disadvantage.

At the end of December, the allied troops crossed the Rhine with the gnawing fear that they would be swallowed up by the plains of Champagne. They could not imagine that the people whose hostility they feared so strongly were too weary to successfully fight them. There would be of course groups of "partisans" who would make life difficult for isolated soldiers; but they would have little influence on the course of the campaign.

Napoleon had put a few marshals, Victor, Marmont and Macdonald, in charge of guarding the frontiers. That was a mistake, for their only desire was to make peace, any peace, which would allow them to put an end to these continuous wars.

The Empire was collapsing like a house of cards. Wellington had crossed the Pyrenees and was advancing in the south; Holland had risen up against

The Battle for the Bridge of Montereau, on February 18, 1814.

The Campaign of France was the most beautiful, and the most desperate, of all the napoleonic campaigns. Napoleon had to confront an adversary superior in number and equipment. But the most formidable obstacle came from within the French ranks: the defection of Murat, betrayal of the old companions. In spite of his continuous victories in the field, Napoleon felt that the possibility of signing any honorable agreement was vanishing. Everything would be decided in Paris, without him, under the leadership of Talleyrand. Jean-Charles Langlois, (1789 - 1870), the Salon of 1840. Musée du château de Versailles.

the French occupying forces and had greeted the Prince of Orange as a saviour; Italy was falling under the control of the Allies, helped by Murat who had entered into an alliance with Austria to save his throne in Naples. Napoleon, convinced that the only satisfying peace he could obtain would be through victory, was persisting in his warlike stance. To his ministers, to his marshals, who were urging him to negotiate, he was replying: *"It is easy to talk of peace,*

but it is not that easy to make it. Europe does not really want it. You believe that we shall disarm Europe by humiliating ourselves before it? You are wrong. The more accommodating you are, the more demanding it will become. Soon it will offer you the frontiers of 1790. We have to fight one more time, to fight a desperate battle. If we are victorious, we shall have to make peace quickly. Rest assured that I shall eagerly participate in the process..."

The Campaign of France was, indeed, desperate. While Paris was plotting his downfall, encouraged by Talleyrand and royalist circles, Napoleon had to confront an adversary superior in number and equipment. All his genius and all the bravery of his "Marie-Louise" could not reverse the situation. The Allies had attacked in winter, whereas Napoleon was expecting them in the spring only. He was sorely lacking the weeks he would have needed to assemble the troops still scattered in Germany and in Spain. The marshals guarding the borders, having lost all will to fight, fell back everywhere without a fight. On January 24, 1814, Napoleon left to join his army and made his farewell to his wife and the little King of Rome. He would never see them again.

The Emperor's arrival strengthened the morale of the troops and of their generals. At one to five, Napoleon undertook to repel the invaders and defeated Blücher's Prussians at Brienne. But the news of Murat's defection was a serious blow to his morale. All his old companions, all those who, for the past 15 years, had been his accomplices in winning and keeping power, were betraying him. How could war be waged with an army whose leaders were demanding negotiations with the enemy?

Napoleon gave in: Caulaincourt was sent to Châtillon to meet with the other side's plenipotentiaries. But that congress was too dependent on the fortunes of war to end in a genuine agreement: each side was hardening or softening its demands according to its military victories or defeats. Aware that his master was risking his throne by refusing the Allies' proposals, Caulaincourt was urging him to accept their demands so as to keep reigning. But whenever Napoleon was finally agreeable to it, it was always too late; victorious, the Allies were no longer granting the conditions still offered the day before.

A risky last manoeuvre to outflank the allied armies failed because of Talleyrand, who had been building up fruitful ties with the royalist circles for several years. His membership in the Council of Regency and his contacts with all the parties made him the arbiter of the situation. Thus Talleyrand, feeling that the empire was lost—he had been working towards that end since 1807—had decided, after much hesitation, to come down in favour of Louis XVIII. Back to France in *"the baggage carriages of the foreigners,"* the brother of Louis XVI was entirely dependent on the Allies' good will for his restoration. The support of the elderly imperial dignitary proved decisive.

Following closely the military operations, Talleyrand made contact with the enemy leaders and, at the crucial moment, sent them one of his agents with a short message: *"You are getting about on crutches, use you legs and go for whatever you can..."*

The defense of Paris: the Clichy Gate, on March 30, 1814.

These are the final hours: the next day, the Czar and the king of Prussia would enter Paris, without a fight; on April 2, Talleyrand would ratify the act deposing the Emperor. Napoleon however was still planning to march on Paris when, on the 4th, his marshals forced him to abdicate.
Horace Vernet (1789 - 1863), dated 1820.
Musée du Louvre.

The Allies understood that France was really exhausted: they marched on Paris. It was the Czar who had especially insisted on taking the capital city, reducing to nothing the Emperor's latest manoeuvre. Paris lost, Marie-Louise having fled to Blois with the Council of Regency (apart from Talleyrand, of course), it was no longer possible to defeat the Allies. After a final attempt to buy time to regroup his troops, Napoleon took refuge in the Château de Fontainebleau

to wait and see how events would turn out. The Czar and the Prussian king entered Paris on March 31, 1814. In compliance with the terms of the capitulation, the city was spared and looting was forbidden. Alexander was experiencing hours of unalloyed happiness and was eager to display his generosity, now that Moscow was symbolically avenged. He was asserting he had waged war against Napoleon, and not against the French people, whom he was quite easily

managing to ingratiate himself with. Frightened and relieved, Paris was oscillating between tears and laughter. Having put his mansion at the Czar's disposal and rekindle the days of Erfurt, Talleyrand had an enormous influence on the russian autocrat's decisions. Napoleon's throne being practically doomed, the most logical possibility then was to put France under the regency of Marie-Louise until the Eaglet comes of age. Such was not the view of the former minister: it was rather advisable, in order to make France forget its past adventures, to restore the former monarchy in all its glory. It was to Louis XVII's advantage that he did not appear fearsome to the Allies, most of whom despised him.

The Czar finally let himself be convinced and asked the Senate to nominate a provisional government. It is as president of this government that Talleyrand, on April 2,1814, ratified the act proclaiming the deposition of the Emperor. But Napoleon was still unresigned. With the arrival of the troops so sorely missed a few days before, he was determined to march on Paris and go for broke. His soldiers were willing to follow him... but not his marshals. On April 4, Macdonald, Lefebvre, Oudinot, Moncey and Ney forced him to renounce the throne. He drafted his declaration of abdication in favor of his son and read it to them.

After finishing, Napoleon looked up, stared at them all and sighed: *"And yet, yet, we would defeat them if we wanted to!"*

Before adding, which was more true: *"I am defeated less by fortune than by the selfishness and the ingratitude of my brothers-in-arms..."*

By proving to the Allies that his marshals were dissociating themselves from their former master, the desertion of Marmont led them to demand an unconditional abdication, which was eliminating the King of Rome from the succession. Napoleon agreed to it, and Louis XVIII was installed. The victors were as generous with the deposed Emperor as they had been with Paris: he was granted complete sovereignty over the island of Elba, he was allowed to retain his imperial title and guaranteed a sum of 2 million francs a year, paid by France... Desperate, Napoleon attempted suicide during the night of April 12 to 13, but he failed: the poison had lost its potency. His fighting spirit soon got the upper hand and he began to make new plans the very next day: see his wife and son again, write his story... And perhaps, make a come back? On April 20, took place the Farewells of Fontainebleau, the farewells to the last followers, to those who had not rallied to the new monarch. Two weeks later, the former Emperor of the Occident landed in the capital of his humble kingdom: Porto Ferrajo.

1815, the imperial leap from the island of Elba to Paris

Two weeks after the Farewells of Fontainebleau, Napoleon landed in Elba. History seemed then to forget him, busy with the Congress of Vienna which opened at the end of September 1814. But the former Emperor, very well informed of the events in France, was still burning to achieve great things. He sailed for the French coast on February 26, 1815. In view of the enthusiastic welcome he was given, he believed that everything was possible again.
Taken from a work by Felix Fleury, Grenoble, 1868.
Taken from a work by Felix Fleury, Grenoble, 1868.

The island of Elba and the Hundred Days: 1814-1815

Thus Louis XVIII was reigning, after twenty-three years of exile. Like the majority of the "Ultras," led by his brother d'Artois, he had neither *"learnt nor forgotten anything."* Reluctant to compromise with his brother's former assassins, covered with silks and gold by the deposed Emperor, the new king intended to exercise a power as absolute as Louis XVI's one. Only the resistance of the Czar and of the imperial dignitaries, who were controlling the State and the Army, could

PATRIE

ILE D'ELBE.

les Gardes de la porte pour le mettre dehors.

Cet homme fera son chemin

Donnez lui des Calottes.

Faisons lui une petite guerre !

convince him to "grant" a Charter to his people. Bulky but quick witted, Louis XVIII knew he would have to compromise. But he was willing to do so only if these momentary concessions were to allow him to restore a strong power. Talleyrand, to whom he owed his return, was provisionally appointed minister, before being sent to Vienna. The first thing to do, even before thinking about reorganizing the country devastated by war and the Allies' occupation, was to conclude a peace treaty with them. It was signed in Paris on May 30, and brought back France to its borders of 1791 to which were added Nice and a part of Savoy. The Coalition reserved the right to dispose of the vast territories abandoned by France. These were to be shared out during the Congress of Vienna which began at the end of September 1814 (the official opening took place on November 1) and ended on June 9, 1815. Talleyrand showed there his diplomatic skills, turning against the Allies the weakness of his position, which was forcing him to neutrality, by advocating the respect of principles. Legitimacy, he said, should be the source and the aim of the new European equilibrium. That simple argument was thwarting the Czar's annexationist aspirations in Poland and Prussia's ones in Saxony.

The Battle of Waterloo

Napoleon's two adversaries at Waterloo were Wellington and Blücher. The Emperor planned to defeat in succession the two armies which were separated. After an initial success of the French troops, Wellington, whose troops had been reinforced by the Prussians just at the right moment, reversed the situation on June 18. Here, the 1st chasseurs, under General Cambronne's command, has formed, at Haie-Sainte, into the last square of the Grande Armée.
Property of Lambert,
n°10, rue Serpente, Paris..
Property of Lambert,
n°10, rue Serpente, Paris.

Thanks to an agreement signed on January 3, 1815, by Austria, France and Great Britain, a war between the Allies was avoided and Alexander yielded. The Prussians had to be satisfied with two fifths of Saxony and Russia with a large part of Poland, while Austria was obtaining compensations in northern Italy and the German Confederation was uniting the German princes.

An unexpected event however disturbed the smooth running of the negotiations: news came at the beginning of March that Napoleon had escaped from the island of Elba. This disturbing news contributed to the immediate reforming of the Coalition, momentarily split by the antagonistic interests of its member states. Although contacted by agents of the Emperor, Talleyrand remained "loyal" to Louis XVIII and drafted himself a declaration whereby the Powers proclaimed that Napoleon was placed outside *"civil and social relations and had delivered himself over to public prosecution as an enemy and a disturber of the peace of the world."*

This text had hardly any impact on the French public, who had sampled Restoration enough to miss the Empire. The humiliated officers put on half pay, the landlords irritated to see the Chamber question the sale of national lands, the bourgeoisie annoyed by the aristocrats' return to power, declared themselves in favour of the Emperor, who was cheered all the way to Paris. It was the start of the "Hundred Days."

The few months spent on the island of Elba had convinced Napoleon that he was not suited to living the life of a minor Italian prince. He needed, to feel totally fulfilled, great designs which the peaceful shores of his island were forbidding. Observing closely the evolution of opinion in France and joyously counting the mistakes of Louis XVIII and of his entourage, he thought that his time could come again. On February 26, 1815, he sailed for the French coast on his final escapade.

"From Cannes to Grenoble I was an adventurer, in this last city, I was again a sovereign"… he will say in St Helena.

On March 19, Louis XVIII had to leave Paris, his government having collapsed because of its incapacity to cope with the crisis. The very next day, which was the Eaglet's birthday, Napoleon entered the capital. All his partisans, in full uniform, were waiting for him at the Tuileries.

"I want peace, announced the Emperor before adding: but it is not only peace I want to give France, it is liberty..."

The whole country rallied around its former master; Louis XVII was forced to leave the territory. Already the army was reorganized and new troops were hastily called up to face the million men converging on the frontiers. The diplomatic offensive, designed to split the Coalition by playing on its divergent interests, came to nothing. The repeated promises made to respect the terms of the Treaty of Paris of May 30, 1814, fell similarly on deaf ears. It was once more necessary to make war. Having learnt from past mistakes, Napoleon showed himself more liberal than ever, restoring full freedom of the press and hoping to become a constitutional monarch. Was he having any other choice, to conquer public opinion, than to show he was a better prince than the Bourbons? He gave Benjamin Constant the task to draft a project of liberal Constitution, called *"Additional Act to the Constitution of the Empire"* in order not to rescind all that had preceded 1814. The method was hardly appreciated: it looked like the ruse of a threatened despot, who would take back once victorious everything he had been forced to give up. Although tired of the arrogance shown by the nobility reinstated with Louis XVIII, the bourgeoisie was loath to favour an Empire which had turned the whole of Europe against it. These industrialists, these merchants, these notabilities, these high ranking civil servants were longing above all for peace. Only the common folk were prepared to follow Napoleon in his war-like adventures. His avowed desire for peace appeared like a pious hope.

Murat, allied to his brother-in-law he had betrayed in 1814, precipitated the war by attacking Austria in Italy. He knew that the Congress of Vienna was getting ready to remove him and he wanted to become master of the peninsula before it was too late. Defeated at Tolentino on May 3, he was forced into exile to escape capture. That defeat deprived Napoleon of a support which could have been effective against Austria in case of a concerted attack.

At the beginning of June, after the "Champ de Mai" where the army, the National Guard and the Imperial Guard swore to perish in the defence of throne and country, the Emperor left for the plains of Flanders to meet the advancing enemy. He knew that it would be

double or quits: victorious he might possibly impose himself on Europe, defeated he would lose everything.

Napoleon's two adversaries for his final campaign were the British Wellington and the Prussian Blücher. The Russians and Austrians did not take part in Waterloo, arriving too late for the battle. As the two enemy armies were separated, the Emperor planned to destroy them in succession.

The Prussians were jostled at Ligny, but Ney, held up by the British, could not intervene in time to rout Blücher. The day finished in a status quo favourable to the French who had cut the Allies off each other. On June 18, it was Waterloo: Wellington,

whose troops were reinforced by the Prussians just at the right moment, was able to resist the French assaults and to reverse the situation in his favour. A hasty attack lead by Ney was unable to pierce the British line; and the Young Guard was being badly mauled by the Prussians. The French forces were soon in compelte disarray, all the more after Wellington's final assault. Only the Guard, formed into a last square, was resisting and suffering heavy losses.

Napoleon wanted to stay and die with his men: why survive that disaster? He will regret later, in St Helena, not to have died there and then. But would his soldiers have possibly accepted to let their god die?

The taking of Alexandria
Kleber wounded

Denon   **Monge**

Bonaparte appointing the Divan of Cairo

Bonaparte and the Envoys of the Monks of Sinaï

Soldats

[Handwritten letter reproduced below in print]

Austerlitz, 12 frimaire an XIV [*3 décembre 1805*].

Soldats !

Je suis content de vous. Vous avez, à la journée d'Austerlitz, justifié tout ce que j'attendais de votre intrépidité; vous avez décoré vos aigles d'une immortelle gloire. Une armée de cent mille hommes, commandée par les empereurs de Russie et d'Autriche, a été en moins de quatre heures, ou coupée ou dispersée. Ce qui a échappé à votre fer s'est noyé dans les lacs. Quarante drapeaux, les étendards de la garde impériale de Russie, cent vingt pièces de canon, vingt généraux, plus de trente mille prisonniers sont le résultat de cette journée à jamais célèbre. Cette infanterie tant vantée, et en nombre supérieur, n'a pu résister à votre choc, et désormais vous n'avez plus de rivaux à redouter. Ainsi, en deux mois, cette troisième coalition a été vaincue et dissoute. La paix ne peut plus être éloignée, mais, comme je l'ai promis à mon peuple avant de passer le Rhin, je ne ferai qu'une paix qui nous donne les garanties et assure les récompenses à nos alliés.

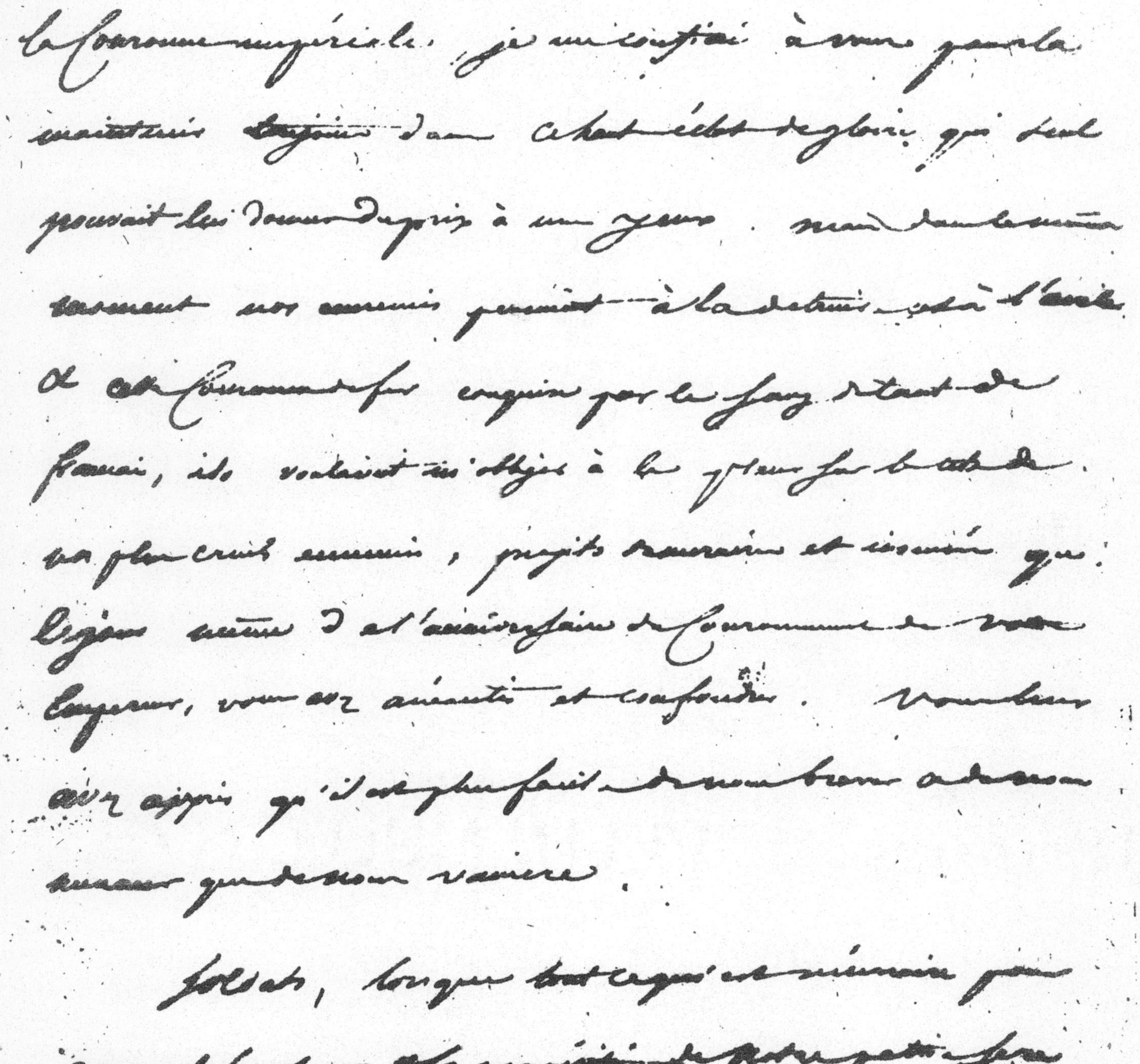

la couronne impériale, je me confiai à vous pour la
maintenir ~~toujours~~ dans cet état éclat de gloire qui seul
pouvait lui donner du prix à mes yeux. mais dans le même
moment nos ennemis pensaient à la détruire et à l'avilir
et cette couronne de fer, conquise par le sang de tant de
français, ils voulaient m'obliger à la placer sur la tête de
nos plus cruels ennemis, projets téméraires et insensés que,
le jour même de l'anniversaire du couronnement de votre
empereur, vous avez anéantis et confondus. vous leur
avez appris qu'il est plus facile de nous braver et de nous
menacer que de nous vaincre.

Soldats, lorsque tout ce qui est nécessaire pour
assurer le bonheur et la prospérité de notre patrie sera
accompli, je vous ramènerai en france; là vous
serez l'objet de mes plus tendres sollicitudes. mon peuple
vous reverra avec joie, et il vous suffira de dire:
j'étais à la bataille d'Austerlitz pour que l'on
réponde: voilà un brave.

De notre camp impérial
d'Austerlitz le 12 février — 14.

Soldats, lorsque le peuple français plaça sur ma tête la couronne impériale, je me confiai à vous pour le maintenir toujours dans ce haut éclat de la gloire qui seul pouvait lui donner du prix à mes yeux. Mais dans le même moment nos ennemis pensaient à la détruire et à l'avilir ! Et cette couronne de fer, conquise par le sang de tant de Français, ils voulaient m'obliger à la placer sur la tête de nos plus cruels ennemis ! Projets téméraires et insensés que, le jour même de l'anniversaire du couronnement de votre Empereur, vous avez anéantis et confondus ! Vous leur avez appris qu'il est plus facile de nous braver et de nous menacer que de nous vaincre.

Soldats, lorsque tout ce qui est nécessaire pour assurer le bonheur et la prospérité de notre patrie sera accompli, je vous ramènerai en France; là vous serez l'objet de mes plus tendres sollicitudes. Mon peuple vous reverra avec joie, et il vous suffira de dire "J'étais à la bataille d'Austerlitz" pour que l'on vous réponde : "Voilà un brave".

Napoléon

117

Egyptian costumes

Louis Bonaparte **Eugène de Beauharnais**

The Eastern Army
Dromedary Regiment

Desaix   ***Mourad-Bey***

NOUVELLES
OFFICIELLES
DE LA GRANDE ARMÉE.
EXTRAIT DU MONITEUR du 9 mai 1813.

Paris, le 8 mai.

Sa majesté l'Impératrice-Reine et Régente a reçu les nouvelles suivantes de l'armée :

Les combats de Weissenfels et de Lutzen n'étaient que le prélude d'événemens de la plus haute importance.

L'empereur Alexandre et le roi de Prusse, qui étaient arrivés à Dresde avec toutes leurs forces dans les derniers jours d'avril, apprenant que l'armée française avait débouché de la Thuringe, adoptèrent le plan de lui livrer bataille dans les plaines de Lutzen, et se mirent en marche pour en occuper la position ; mais ils furent prévenus par la rapidité des mouvemens de l'armée française ; ils persistèrent cependant dans leurs projets, et résolurent d'attaquer l'armée pour la déposter des positions qu'elle avait prises.

La position de l'armée française au 2 mai, à neuf heures du matin, était la suivante :

La gauche de l'armée s'appuyait à l'Elster ; elle était formée par le vice-roi, ayant sous ses ordres les 5e et 11e corps. Le centre était commandé par le prince de la Moskowa, au village de Kaïa. L'Empereur avec la jeune et la vieille garde était à Lutzen.

Le duc de Raguse était au défilé de Poserna, et formait la droite avec ses trois divisions. Enfin le général Bertrand, commandant le 4e corps, marchait pour se rendre à ce défilé. L'ennemi débouchait et passait l'Elster aux ponts de Zwenkau, Pegau et Zeitz. S. M. ayant l'espérance de le prévenir dans son mouvement, et pensant qu'il ne pourrait attaquer que le 3, ordonna au général Lauriston, dont le corps formait l'extrêmité de la gauche, de se porter sur Leipsick, afin de déconcerter les projets de l'ennemi et de placer l'armée française, pour la journée du 3, dans une position toute différente de celle où les ennemis avaient compté la trouver et où elle été effectivement le 2, et de porter ainsi de la confusion et du désordre dans leurs colonnes.

A 9 heures du matin, S. M. ayant entendu une canonnade du côté de Leipsick, s'y porta au galop. L'ennemi défendait le petit village de Listenau et les ponts en avant de Leipsick. S. M. n'attendait que le moment où ces dernières positions seraient enlevées, pour mettre en mouvement toute son armée dans cette direction, la faire pivoter sur Leipsick, passer sur la droite de l'Elster, et prendre l'ennemi à revers; mais à dix heures, l'ormée ennemie déboucha vers Kaïa sur plusieurs colonnes d'une noire profondeur, l'horizon en était obscurci.

L'ennemi présentait des forces qui paraissaient immenses : l'Empereur fit sur-le-champ ses dispositions. Le vice-roi reçut l'ordre de se porter sur la gauche du prince de la Moskowa, mais il lui fallait trois heures pour exécuter ce mouvement. Le prince de la Moskowa prit les armes, et avec ses cinq divisions soutint le combat, qui au bout d'une demi-heure devint terrible. S. M. se porta elle-même à la tête de la garde derrière le centre de l'armée, soutenant la droite du prince de la Moskowa. Le duc de Raguse, avec ses trois divisions, occupait l'extrême droite.

Le général Bertrand eut ordre de déboucher sur les derrières de l'armée ennemie, au moment où la ligne se trouverait le plus fortement engagée.

La fortune se plut à couronner du plus brillant succès toutes ces dispositions. L'ennemi, qui paraissait certain de la réussite de son entreprise, marchait pour déborder notre droite et gagner le chemin de Weissenfels. Le général Compans, général de bataille du premier mérite, à la tête de la 1re division du duc de Raguse, l'arrêta tout court.

Les régimens de marine soutinrent plusieurs charges avec sang-froid, et couvrirent le champ de bataille de l'élite de la cavalerie ennemie. Mais les grands efforts d'infanterie, d'artillerie et de cavalerie, étaient sur le centre. Quatre des cinq divisions du prince de la Moskowa étaient déjà engagées. Le village Kaïa fut pris et repris plusieurs fois. Ce village était resté au pouvoir de l'ennemi : le comte de Lobau dirigea le général Ricard pour reprendre le village; il fut repris.

La bataille embrassait une ligne de deux lieues couvertes de feu, de fumée et de tourbillons de poussière. Le prince de la Moskowa, le général Souham, le général Girard, étaient partout, faisaient face à tout. Blessé de plusieurs balles, le général Girard voulut rester sur-le-champ de bataille. Il déclara vouloir mourir en commandant et dirigeant ses troupes, puisque le moment était arrivé pour tous les français qui avaient du cœur, de vaincre ou de périr.

Cependant, on commençait à apercevoir dans le lointain la poussière et les premiers feux du corps du général Bertrand. Au même moment le vice-roi entrait en ligne sur la gauche, et le duc de Tarente attaquait la réserve de l'ennemi, et abordait au village où l'ennemi appuyait sa droite. Dans ce moment, l'ennemi redoubla ses efforts sur le centre; le village de Kaïa fut emporté de nouveau; notre centre fléchit; quelques bataillons se débandèrent; mais cette valeureuse jeunesse , à la vue de l'Empereur , se rallia en criant : vive l'Empereur !

S. M. jugea que le moment de crise qui décide du gain ou de la perte des batailles était arrivé : il n'y avait plus un moment à perdre. L'Empereur ordonna au duc de Trévise de se porter avec seize bataillons de la jeune garde au village de Kaïa, de donner tête baissée, de culbuter l'ennemi, de reprendre le village , et de faire main-basse sur tout ce qui s'y trouvait.

Au même moment S. M. ordonna à son aide-de-camp le général Drouot, officier d'artillerie de la plus grande distinction , de réunir une batterie de 80 pièces; et de la placer en avant de la vieille garde , qui fut disposée en échelons comme quatre redoutes , pour soutenir le centre, toute notre cavalerie rangée en bataille derrière.

Les généraux Dulauloy, Drouot et Devaux partirent au galop avec leurs 80 bouches à feu placées en un même groupe. Le feu devint épouvantable. L'ennemi fléchit de tous côtés. Le duc de Trévise emporta sans coup férir le village de Kaïa, culbuta l'ennemi, et continua à se porter en avant en battant la charge. Cavalerie , infanterie, artillerie de l'ennemi, tout se mit en retraite.

Le général Bonnet, commandant une division du duc de Raguse, reçut ordre de faire un mouvement par sa gauche sur Kaïa, pour appuyer les succès du centre. Il soutint plusieurs charges de cavalerie dans lesquelles l'ennemi éprouva de grandes pertes.

Cependant le général comte Bertrand s'avançait et entrait en ligne. C'est en vain que la cavalerie ennemie caracola autour de ses quarrés ; sa marche n'en fut pas ralentie : pour le rejoindre plus promptement, l'Empereur ordonna un changement de direction en pivotant sur Kaïa. Toute la droite fit un changement de front, la droite en avant.

L'ennemi ne fit plus que fuir; nous le poursuivîmes une lieue et demie. Nous arrivâmes bientôt sur la hauteur que l'empereur Alexandre, le roi de Prusse et la famille de Brandebourg y occupaient pendant la bataille. Un officier prisonnier qui se trouvait là , nous apprit cette circonstance.

Nous avons fait plusieurs milliers de prisonniers. Le nombre n'a pu en être plus considérable, vu l'infériorité de notre cavalerie, et le désir que l'Empereur avait montré de l'épargner.

Au commencement de la bataille, l'Empereur avait dit aux troupes : « C'est une bataille d'Egypte. Une bonne infanterie, « soutenue par l'artillerie, doit savoir se suffire. »

Le général Gourré, chef d'état-major du prince de la Moskowa, a été tué, mort digne d'un si bon soldat! Notre perte se monte à 10,000 tués ou blessés. Celle de l'ennemi peut être évaluée de 25 à 30,000 hommes. La garde royale de Prusse a été détruite. Les gardes de l'Empereur de Russie ont considérablement souffert : les deux divisions de dix régimens de cuirassiers russes ont été écrasées.

S. M. ne saurait trop faire l'éloge de la bonne volonté, du courage et de l'intrépidité de l'armée. Nos jeunes soldats ne considéraient pas le danger. Ils ont dans cette grande circonstance relevé toute la noblesse du sang français.

L'état-major-général, dans sa relation, fera connaître les belles actions qui ont illustré cette brillante journée, qui, comme un coup de tonnerre, a pulvérisé les chimériques espérances et tous les calculs de destruction et de démembrement de l'empire. Les trames ténébreuses ourdies par le cabinet de Saint-James pendant tout un hiver, se trouvent en un instant dénouées comme le nœud gordien par l'épée d'Alexandre.

Le prince de Hesse-Hombourg a été tué. Les prisonniers disent que le jeune prince royal de Prusse a été blessé, et que le prince de Mecklenbourg-Strelitz a été tué.

L'infanterie de la vieille garde, dont six bataillons étaient seulement arrivés, a soutenu par sa présence l'affaire avec ce sang-froid qui la caractérise. Elle n'a pas tiré un coup de fusil. La moitié de l'armée n'a pas donné, car les quatre divisions du corps du général Lauriston n'ont fait qu'occuper Leipsick; les trois divisions du duc de Reggio étaient encore à deux journées du champ de bataille; le comte Bertrand n'a donné qu'avec une de ses divisions, et si légèrement, qu'elle n'a pas perdu 50 hommes; ses seconde et troisième divisions n'ont pas donné.

La seconde division de la jeune garde, commandée par le général Barrois, était encore à cinq journées; il en est de même de la moitié de la vieille garde, commandée par le général Decouz, qui n'était encore qu'à Erfurth : des batteries de réserve formant plus de 100 bouches à feu n'avaient pas rejoint, et elles sont encore en marche depuis Mayence jusqu'à Erfurth; le corps du duc de Bellune était aussi à trois jours du champ de bataille.

Le corps de cavalerie du général Sébastiani, avec les trois divisions du prince d'Eckmülh, étaient du côté du Bas-Elbe. L'armée alliée forte de 150 à 200,000 hommes, commandée par les deux souverains, ayant un grand nombre de princes de la maison de Prusse à sa tête, a donc été défaite et mise en déroute par moins de la moitié de l'armée française.

Les ambulances et le champ de bataille offraient le spectacle le plus touchant : les jeunes soldats, à la vue de l'Empereur, faisaient trève à leur douleur en criant vive l'Empereur. — « Il y a vingt ans, a dit l'Empereur, « que je commande des armées françaises : je n'ai pas encore vu autant de « bravoure et de dévouement. »

L'Europe serait enfin tranquille si les souverains et les ministres qui dirigent leur cabinet pouvaient avoir été présent sur ce champ de bataille. Ils renonceraient à l'espérance de faire rétrograder l'étoile de la France; ils verraient que les conseillers qui veulent démembrer l'empire français et humilier l'Empereur préparent la perte de leurs souverains.

De l'imprimerie du JOURNAL DE PARIS, pour lequel on s'abonne, rue de la Monnaie, n° 11.

Proclamation de l'Empereur à l'armée.

« Soldats, je suis content de vous ! vous avez rempli mon at-
« tente ! vous avez suppléé à tout par votre bonne volonté et par
« votre bravoure. Vous avez, dans la célèbre journée du 2 mai, défait
« et mis en déroute l'armée russe et prussienne commandée par
« l'empereur Alexandre et par le roi de Prusse. Vous avez ajouté
« un nouveau lustre à la gloire de mes aigles : vous avez montré
« tout ce dont est capable le sang français.

« La bataille de Lutzen sera mise au-dessus des batailles d'Aus-
« terlitz, d'Jéna, de Friedland et de la Moskowa ! Dans la campagne
« passée, l'ennemi n'a trouvé de refuge contre nos armes qu'en sui-
« vant la méthode féroce des barbares ses ancêtres. Des armées de
« tartares ont incendié ses campagnes, ses villes, la sainte Moscou
« elle-même !

« Aujourd'hui ils arrivaient dans nos contrées, précédés de
» tout ce que l'Allemagne, la France et l'Italie ont de mauvais
» sujets et de déserteurs, pour y prêcher la révolte, l'anarchie,
» la guerre civile, le meurtre. Ils se sont faits les apôtres de
» tous les crimes. C'est un incendie moral qu'ils voulaient allu-
» mer entre la Vistule et le Rhin, pour, selon l'usage des
» gouvernemens despotiques, mettre des déserts entre nous et
» eux.

» Les insensés ! ils connaissaient peu l'attachement à leurs
» souverains, la sagesse, l'esprit d'ordre et le bon sens des
» Allemands ! Ils connaissaient peu la puissance et la bravoure
» des Français !

» Dans une seule journée, vous avez déjoué tous ces com-
» plots parricides… Nous rejetterons ces Tartares dans leurs
» affreux climats qu'ils ne doivent pas franchir.

» Qu'ils restent dans leurs déserts glacés, séjour d'escla-
» vage, de barbarie et de corruption où l'homme est ravalé à
» l'égal de la brute. Vous avez bien mérité de l'Europe civi-
» lisé ; soldats ! l'Italie, la France, l'Allemagne vous rendent
» des actions de graces !

» De notre camp impérial de Lutzen, le 3 mai 1813.
» Signé NAPOLÉON.

NOUVELLES
DE LA
GRANDE ARMÉE.

SITUATION DE L'ARMÉE AU SEIZE OCTOBRE.

Sa Majesté l'Impératrice-Reine et Régente a reçu les nouvelles suivantes :

Le 15, le prince Schwarzenberg, commandant l'armée ennemie, annonça à l'ordre du jour, que le lendemain 16, il y aurait une bataille générale et décisive. Effectivement le 16, à 9 heures du matin, la grande armée alliée déboucha sur nous. Elle opérait constamment pour s'étendre sur sa droite. On vit d'abord trois grosses colonnes se porter, l'une le long de la rivière de l'Elster, contre le village de Dœlitz; la seconde contre le village de Wachau, et la troisième contre celui de Liberwolkowitz. Ces trois colonnes étaient précédées par deux cents pièces de canon. L'Empereur fit aussitôt ses dispositions. A 10 heures, la canonnade était des plus fortes, et à 11 heures les deux armées étaient engagées aux villages de Dœlitz, Wachau et Liberwolkowitz. Ces villages furent attaqués six à sept fois; l'ennemi fut constamment repoussé et couvrit les avenues de ses cadavres.

Le comte Lauriston, avec le 5.e corps, défendait le village de gauche (Liberwolkowitz); le prince Poniatowski, avec ses braves Polonais, défendait le village de droite (Dœlitz), et le duc de Bellune défendait Wachau. A midi, la 6.e attaque de l'ennemi avait été repoussée, nous étions maitres des trois villages, et nous avions fait deux mille prisonniers. A peu près au même moment, le duc de Tarente débouchait par Holzhausen, se portant sur une redoute de l'ennemi, que le général Charpentier enleva au pas de charge, en s'emparant de l'artillerie et faisant quelques prisonniers. Le moment parut décisif. L'empereur ordonna au duc de Reggio de se porter sur Wachau avec deux divisions de la jeune garde. Il ordonna également au duc de Trévise de se porter sur Liberwolkowitz avec deux autres divisions de la jeune garde et de s'emparer d'un grand bois, qui est sur la gauche du village. En même-tems, il fit avancer sur le centre une batterie de 150 pièces de canon, que dirigea le général Drouot.

L'ensemble de ces dispositions eut le succès qu'on en attendait. L'artillerie ennemie s'éloigna. L'ennemi se retira et le champ de bataille nous resta tout entier.

Il était trois heures après-midi. Toutes les troupes de l'ennemi avaient été engagées. Il eut recours à sa réserve. Le comte de Merfeld, qui commandait en chef la réserve autrichienne , releva avec six divisions toutes les troupes sur toutes les attaques, et la garde impériale russe, qui formait la réserve de l'armée russe, les releva au centre.

La cavalerie de la garde russe et les cuirassiers autrichiens se précipitèrent par leur gauche sur notre droite, s'emparèrent de Dœlitz et vinrent caracoller autour des carrés du duc de Bellune. Le roi de Naples marcha avec les cuirassiers de Latour-Maubourg, et chargea la cavalerie ennemie par la gauche de Wachau, dans le tems que la cavalerie polonaise et les dragons de la garde, commandés par le général Letort, chargeaient par la droite. La cavalerie ennemie fut défaite; deux régimens entiers restèrent sur le champ de bataille. Le général Letort fit 300 prisonniers russes et autrichiens. Le général Latour-Maubourg pris quelques centaines d'hommes de la garde russe.

L'Empereur fit sur-le-champ avancer la division Curial de la garde, pour renforcer le prince Poniatowski. Le général Curial se porta au village de Dœlitz, l'attaqua à la bayonnette, le prit sans coup férir et fit 1200 prisonniers, parmi lesquels s'est trouvé le général en chef Merfeld.

Les affaires ainsi rétablies à notre droite, l'ennemi se mit en retraite, et le champ de bataille ne nous fut pas disputé. Les pièces de la réserve de la garde que commandait le général Drouot, étaient avec les tirailleurs, la cavalerie ennemie vint les charger. Les canonniers rangèrent en carré leurs pièces, qu'ils avaient eu la précaution de charger à mitraille, et tirèrent avec tant d'agilité qu'en un instant l'ennemi fut repoussé. Sur ces entrefaites la cavalerie française s'avança pour soutenir ces batteries. Le général Maison, commandant une division du 5.e corps, officier de la plus grande distinction, fut blessé. Le général Latour-Maubourg, commandant la cavalerie eut la cuisse emportée d'un boulet. Notre perte dans cette journée a été de 2,500 hommes, tant tués que blessés. Ce n'est pas exa-

gérer que de porter celle de l'ennemi à 25,000 hommes. On ne saurait trop faire l'éloge de la conduite du comte Lauriston et du prince Poniatowski dans cette journée. Pour donner à ce dernier une preuve de sa satisfaction, l'Empereur l'a nommé sur le champ de bataille maréchal de France, et a accordé un grand nombre de décorations aux régimens de son corps.

Le général Bertrand était en même tems attaqué au village de Lindenau par les généraux Giulay, Thielman et Liechtenstein. On déploya de part et d'autre une cinquantaine de pièces de canon. Le combat dura six heures sans que l'ennemi pût gagner un pouce de terrain. A cinq heures du soir, le général Bertrand décida la victoire en faisant une charge avec sa réserve, et non-seulement il rendit vains les projets de l'ennemi, qui voulait s'emparer des ponts de Lindenau et des faubourgs de Leipsick; mais encore il le contraignit à évacuer son champ de bataille.

Sur la droite de la Partha, à une lieue de Leipsick, et à-peu-près à quatre lieues du champ de bataille où se trouvait l'Empereur, le duc de Raguse fut engagé. Par une de ces circonstances fatales, qui influent souvent sur les affaires les plus importantes, le 3.e corps qui devait soutenir le duc de Raguse, n'entendant rien de ce côté, à dix heures du matin, et entendant au contraire une effroyable canonnade du côté où se trouvait l'Empereur, crut bien faire de s'y porter, et perdit ainsi sa journée en marches.

Le duc de Raguse, livrés à ses propres forces, défendit Leipsick et soutint sa position pendant toute la journée; mais il éprouva des pertes, qui n'ont point été compensées par celles qu'il a fait éprouver à l'ennemi, quelques grandes qu'elles fussent. Des bataillons de canonniers de la marine se sont faiblement comportés. Les généraux Compans et Frederichs ont été blessés.

Le soir, le duc de Raguse, légèrement blessé lui-même, a été obligé de resserrer sa position sur la Partha. Il a dû abandonner dans ce mouvement plusieurs pièces démontées et plusieurs voitures.

Pour copie conforme : *L'Auditeur au Conseil d'Etat, Préfet du Département de la Vendée ,*

Le Baron de CHATEAUBOURG.

ez ALLUT Imprimeur de la Préfecture, du Journal Politique et des Annonces Judiciaires du Département.

NOUVELLES OFFICIELLES

DE LA GRANDE-ARMÉE.

SITUATION DE L'ARMÉE AU VINGT MARS.

Sa Majesté l'Impératrice-Reine et Régente a reçu les nouvelles suivantes :

Le général russe Wittgenstein, avec son corps d'armée, était à Villenoxe. Il avait jeté des ponts à Pont, où il avait passé la Seine, et il marchait sur Provins.

Le duc de Tarente avait réuni ses troupes sur cette ville. Le 16, l'ennemi manœuvrait pour déborder sa gauche. Le duc de Reggio engagea son artillerie, et toute la journée se passa en canonnade. Le mouvement de l'ennemi paraissait se prononcer sur Provins et sur Nangis.

D'un autre côté, le prince de Schwartzenberg, l'empereur Alexandre et le roi de Prusse, étaient à Arcis-sur-Aube.

Le corps du prince-royal de Wurtemberg s'était porté sur Villers-aux-Corneilles.

Le général Platow, avec ses trois mille barbares, s'était jeté sur Fère-Champenoise et Sézanne.

L'empereur d'Autriche venait d'arriver de Chaumont à Troyes.

Le prince de la Moskowa est entré le 16 à Châlons-sur-Marne.

L'Empereur a couché le 17 à Epernai, le 18 à Fère-Champenoise, et le 19 à Plancy.

Le général Sébastiani, à la tête de sa cavalerie, a rencontré à Fère-Champenoise le général Platow, l'a culbuté et l'a poursuivi jusqu'à l'Aube, en lui faisant des prisonniers.

Le 19, après-midi, l'Empereur a passé l'Aube à Plancy. A cinq heures du soir, il a passé la Seine à un gué et fait tourner Méry, qui a été occupé.

A sept heures du soir, le général Letort, avec les chasseurs de la Garde, est arrivé au village de Châtres coupant la route de Nogent à Troyes ; mais l'ennemi était déjà par-tout en retraite. Cependant le général Letort a pu atteindre son parc de pontons, qui avait servi à faire le pont de Pont-sur-Seine ; il s'est emparé de tous les pontons sur leurs haquets attelés, et d'une centaine de voitures de bagages ; il a fait des prisonniers.

Dans la journée du 17, le général Wrede avait rétrogradé rapidement sur Arcis-sur-Aube. Dans la nuit du 17 au 18, l'empereur de Russie s'était retiré sur Troyes. Le 18, les Souverains alliés ont évacué Troyes et se sont portés, en toute hâte, sur Bar-sur-Aube.

S. M. l'Empereur est arrivé à Arcis-sur-Aube le 20 au matin.

Pour copie conforme : *l'Auditeur au Conseil d'Etat, Préfet du Département de la Vendée,*

LE BARON DE CHATEAUBOURG.

A NAPOLÉON, chez ALLUT, Imprimeur de la Préfecture.

NOUVELLES OFFICIELLES

DE LA GRANDE-ARMÉE.

SITUATION DE L'ARMÉE AU VINGT-NEUF MARS.

SA Majesté l'Impératrice-Reine et Régente a reçu des nouvelles des Armées :

Le général de division Piré est entré à Chaumont, le 5 mars, et a ainsi coupé la ligne d'opération de l'ennemi. Il a intercepté beaucoup de courriers et d'estafettes, a enlevé à l'ennemi des bagages, plusieurs pièces de canon, ses magasins d'habillement et une grande partie de ses hôpitaux, il a été parfaitement secondé par les habitans de la campagne qui sont partout en armes et montrent la plus grande ardeur.

M. le baron de Vessenberg, ministre d'Autriche en Angleterre, revenant de Londres avec le comte Palfi, son secrétaire de légation; le lieutenant-général suédois Schiol de Brand, ministre de Suède auprès de l'Empereur de Russie avec un major suédois; le conseiller de guerre prussien Piguielhen, MM. Tolstoy et de Marcoff, et des officiers d'ordonnance russes, allant tous en mission aux différens quartiers-généraux des alliés, ont été arrêtés par les levées en masse et conduits au quartier-général. L'enlèvement de ces personnages, et de leurs papiers qui ont été pris, est d'une grande importance.

Le parc de l'armée russe et tous les équipages étaient à Bar-sur-Aube, à la première nouvelle des mouvemens de l'armée, ils ont été évacués sur Béfort, ce qui prive l'ennemi de ses munitions d'artillerie et de transport de vivres de réserve qui lui étaient nécessaires.

L'armée ennemie ayant pris le parti d'opérer entre l'Aube et la Marne, avait laissé le général Russe Witzingerode à Saint-Dizier, avec 8000 hommes de cavalerie et deux divisions d'infanterie, afin de maintenir la ligne d'opération et de faciliter l'arrivée de l'artillerie, des munitions et des vivres dont l'ennemi a le plus grand besoin.

La division de dragons du général Milhaud et la cavalerie de la Garde commandée par le général Sébastiani, ont passé le gué de Valcour le 26 mars, ont marché sur cette cavalerie et après de belles charges l'ont mise en déroute. Trois mille hommes de la cavalerie russe dont beaucoup de la garde impériale, ont été tués ou pris, les 18 pièces de canon qu'avait l'ennemi lui ont été enlevées ainsi que ses bagages. L'ennemi a laissé les bois et les prairies jonchées de ses morts. Tous les corps de cavalerie se sont distingués à l'envi les uns des autres.

Le duc de Reggio a poursuivi l'ennemi jusqu'à Bar-sur-Ornain.

Le 29, le quartier-général de l'Empereur était à Troyes. Des convois de prisonniers dont le nombre s'élève à plus de 6000 suivent l'armée.

Dans tous les villages, les habitans sont sous les armes, exaspérés par les violences, les crimes et les ravages de l'ennemi. Ils lui font une guerre acharnée qui est pour lui du plus grand danger.

L'Empereur qui avait porté son quartier-général à Troyes le 29, s'est dirigé à marches forcées par Sens sur la Capitale; mais l'ennemi y était entré. L'occupation de Paris par l'ennemi est un malheur qui afflige profondément le cœur de Sa Majesté et de tous les bons Français; mais dont il ne faut pas concevoir d'allarmes. La présence de l'Empereur avec son armée aux portes de Paris, empêchera l'ennemi de se porter à ses excès accoutumés dans une ville si populeuse, qu'il ne saurait garder sans rendre sa position dangereuse. Elle l'empêchera aussi de détacher autre chose que des troupes légères, pour inquiéter les départemens voisins.

Pour copie conforme : *L'Auditeur au Conseil d'Etat, Préfet du Département de la Vendée,*

LE BARON DE CHATEAUBOURG.

A NAPOLÉON, chez ALLUT, Imprimeur de la Préfecture.

PROCLAMATION.

S. M. L'IMPÉRATRICE-REINE
ET RÉGENTE
A TOUS LES FRANÇAIS.

FRANÇAIS,

LES événemens de la guerre ont mis la Capitale au pouvoir de l'Etranger.

L'Empereur, accouru pour la défendre, est à la tête de ses Armées si souvent victorieuses.

Elles sont en présence de l'ennemi sous les murs de Paris.

C'est de la résidence que j'ai choisie, et des Ministres de l'Empereur, qu'émaneront les seuls ordres que vous puissiez reconnaître.

Toute ville, au pouvoir de l'ennemi, cesse d'être libre, toute direction qui en émane, est le langage de l'étranger, ou celui qu'il convient à ses vues hostiles de propager.

Vous serez fidèles à vos sermens. Vous écouterez la voix d'une Princesse qui s'est remise à votre foi, qui fait toute sa gloire d'être Française, d'être associée aux destinées du Souverain que vous avez librement choisi.

Mon Fils était moins sûr de vos cœurs aux tems de nos prospérités.

Ses droits et sa personne sont sous votre sauve-garde.

Blois 3 Avril 1814

MARIE - LOUISE.

Par l'Impératrice - Régente :

Le Ministre de l'Intérieur, faisant fonctions de Secrétaire de la Régence,

MONTALIVET.

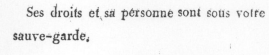

Le Préfet du Département de la Vendée, Auditeur au Conseil d'Etat, Baron de l'Empire,

ARRÊTE

Que la présente Proclamation sera imprimée, lue, publiée et affichée dans toutes les Communes du Département, à la diligence de MM. les Maires.

Napoléon, le 9 Avril 1814.

LE BARON DE CHATEAUBOURG.

NAPOLÉON, chez ALLUT, Imprimeur de la Préfecture, et des Journaux du Département.

EPILOGUE

1815-1821...

St Helena

It was not Talleyrand who pulled the strings of the second abdication, but his old accomplice Fouché. He controlled most of the deputies and ordered them to put pressure on Napoleon to renounce the throne. The Emperor abdicated thus in favor of the "Eaglet" (on June 22), who was proclaimed Emperor under the title of Napoleon II, while Fouché was working towards the return of Louis XVIII.

Napoleon, who had sought refuge in Malmaison, then in Rochefort where he learnt that his passports to America had been refused, put his fate into the hands, he believed magnanimous, of Great Britain. He was compelled to do so by the manoeuvres of Fouché who was planning to hand him over to the royalists. They would probably have sentenced him to death had they been able to capture him.

The British leaders were unwilling to "house" the former Emperor less than a few hundred miles off the coasts of Europe. St Helena, an island in the South Atlantic which had been already considered in 1814, was chosen for Napoleon's exile. At the time when Louis XVIII was getting back his throne with the close support of the Allies, the vanquished was boarding the Northumberland for the island that would become his resting place.

He was to spend six years there, from 1815 to 1821. Surrounded with a few companions, including Bertrand, Gourgaud, Montholon and of course Las Cases, he was able to meditate at length there on his extraordinary destiny. Guarded by 600 cannons, 7 ships and 300 men, Napoleon spent dreary days in the same idleness he suffered so much from while in Elba. His warden, Hudson Lowe, was a subordinate obsessed with regulations who was making his captivity even more miserable.

He soothed his despair by dictating his memoirs to Gourgaud or confiding in Las Cases. After their departure, Bertrand and Montholon remained his only companions. But only death would release him from captivity and he knew it. He had hoped at the beginning that his faithful followers who had migrated to America could free him. That illusion had been quickly dispelled.

Alone, deprived of that glory that had so much illuminated his life, the former Emperor of the Occident, the former adventurer of the Revolution passed away sadly on May 5, 1821.

His death marked the end of an epic, and the birth of a legend the brilliant images of which would fascinate the world and give a meaning to the past.

The Legend

Although the legend of Napoleon was not born on St Helena, it is there that it took its definitive form. The epic tales attached to Napoleon's doings, which started in the plains of Lombardy in 1796 and were magnified by many victories and by the imperial consecration of their hero, would come into full blossom after his death only.

Le Mémorial, published by Las Cases in 1823, would be the temple built by Bonaparte for Napoleon. The deposed Emperor would also benefit from the social and economic crisis that followed the Empire, making that period appear like a golden age, when the government was paying special attention to pensions and to the price of bread, when the currency was stable, inflation contained and salaries decent.

Demobilized and back in their villages, the former soldiers of the Grande Armée would strive to keep their prestige by dedicating a special cult to the souvenir of the grandest hours of the Empire. Those letters they had sent from all over Europe to their families were their strongest arguments. The younger generations, who had grown up in peaceful but economically difficult times, listened to them speak with veneration of the "Little Corporal" while evoking distant and glorious places: Arcole, the Pyramids, Spain, Moscow... The miseries and the weaknesses of the Empire and of its ruler were gradually fading away; only remained the formidable image of a man who had subdued the kingdoms of Europe.

The napoleonic legend was also created by the Romanticism of this first half of the nineteenth century. Writers soon opposed the undeniable grandeur of the imperial epic and the daily mediocrity, the meanness of the bourgeoisie's ambitions. The tragic destiny of this adventurer of the revolution turned visionary conqueror, who died far away from everything on a dreadful volcanic rock, fired the imagination and became permanently engraved on the people's memory.

Through singers, like the famous Béranger, but also through writers such as Lamartine, Musset, Vigny, Hugo or Dumas, the gilded legend would soon erase cruel memories. Stendhal, a late convert himself, would also contribute to the creation of the myth by starting The Charterhouse of Parma with these words:"On May 15, 1796, General Bonaparte entered Milan at the head of that young army which had just crossed the bridge of Lodi and taught the world that after so many centuries Caesar and Alexander had a successor..."

The story book of life was again opening out on to Adventure.

MORT DE BUONAPARTE.

Extrait du Moniteur Universel, du 7 Juillet 1821.

ON a reçu par voie extraordinaire les journaux Anglais du 4 courant.

La mort de Buonaparte y est officiellement annoncée. Voici dans quels termes le *Courrier* donne cette nouvelle :

« Buonaparte n'est plus : il est mort le samedi 5 mai, à six heures du soir, « d'une maladie de langueur qui le retenait au lit depuis plus de 40 jours ».

« Il a demandé qu'après sa mort son corps fût ouvert, afin de reconnaître si « sa maladie n'était pas la même que celle qui avait terminé les jours de son père, « c'est-à-dire, un cancer à l'estomac. L'ouverture du cadavre a prouvé qu'il ne « s'était pas trompé dans ses conjectures. Il a conservé sa connaissance jusqu'au « dernier jour, et il est mort sans douleur.

Voici l'extrait d'une lettre que nous avons sous les yeux ; elle est datée de Sainte-Hélène, le 7 Mai :

« Buonaparte est mort samedi 5 Mai, après une maladie de six semaines, « qui n'avait pris un caractère sérieux que dans la deuxième quinzaine. Le cancer « qui lui rongeait l'estomac avait produit une large ulcération ».

« Il a été exposé depuis hier au soir, après que l'Amiral, le Gouverneur et « autres Autorités eurent visité le corps ».

Quoique sa maladie ne se fût pas prononcée d'abord d'une manière alarmante, « il sentait qu'il n'en pouvait revenir. Bientôt les médecins en furent eux-mêmes « persuadés.

« On dit que, cinq ou six heures avant de mourir, il a donné des instructions « relativement à ses affaires et à ses papiers. Il a demandé à être ouvert afin « que son fils pût être informé de la nature de sa maladie. L'ouverture a été « faite par son propre médecin ».

« Nous croyons qu'il a laissé un testament, qui, avec tous ses autres papiers, « sera envoyé en Angleterre ».

Les dépêches concernant cet événement ont été apportées par le capitaine Crokat, du 20ᵉ régiment. Elles ont été aussitôt communiquées à tous les Ministres et aux Ambassadeurs, qui ont sur-le-champ expédié des courriers à leurs Cours respectives.

Il a fait appeler, avant de mourir, un Ministre de la Religion.

Le journal *The Courrier* en date du 15 mai, rapporte :

« Buonaparte a été enterré le 9 dans la vallée de Sane, qu'il avait désignée « lui-même. Le cercueil était porté par des grenadiers ; MM. Bertrand et Montholon « portaient le poile ; madame Bertrand suivait avec tous ses enfants. La marche était « fermée par ladi Lowe, femme du gouverneur, accompagnée de ses filles, comme « elle en grand deuil. Les collines étaient couronnées par trois mille hommes de « troupes de terre ou de mer ; au moment où le cercueil a été mis en terre, onze « pièces de canon ont tiré trois salves. Il était né le 15 août 1769.

A Beziers, de l'Imprimerie de J.-J. FUZIER.